G000078466

DOMINIQUE PERRAULT ARCHITECT

Birkhäuser - Publishers for Architecture
Basel · Boston · Berlin
ACTAR Barcelona

DOMINIQUE PERRAULT ARCHITECT

Publishers
ACTAR, Barcelona
Birkhäuser –
Publishers for Architecture,
Basel, Boston, Berlin

Concept
Ramon Prat, Albert Ferré,
Gaëlle Lauriot-Prévost

Documentation
Gaëlle Lauriot-Prévost,
Natalie Plágaro Cowee

Text editing
Albert Ferré, Frédéric Migayrou

Translation
Paul Hammond
Naoko Tarasaki (p. 80-84)
Hildi Hawkins (p. 95-97)

Layout
Ramon Prat
David Lorente

**Digitalization and manipulation
of images**
César Cendán, Oriol Rigat,
Sebastià Sànchez

Production
Font i Prat Ass.

Printing
Ingoprint SA, Barcelona

Distribution
Birkhäuser–Publishers for
Architecture
P.O.Box 133
CH-4010 Basel
Tel. +41/61/2050-707
Fax +41/61/2050-792
e-mail: sales@birkhauser.ch
http://www.birkhauser.ch

**ACTAR, Birkhäuser and the office of
Dominique Perrault would like to
thank the following persons and
institutions for their collaboration:**
Mr. Bourillon, SAGEP water
treatment plant.
Richard Copans, Les Filmes d'Ici.
Marie-Anne Escalet, José Gadbois.
Georges Fessy.
Lluís Hortet, Fundació Mies van
der Rohe.
Thierry Louvieaux.
Mr. Martin, Usinor-Sacilor.
Gerardo Mingo Pinacho.
André Morin.
OSB Sportstättenbauten GmbH.
Perrault Projets.
Sylvie Soulignac, Bibliothèque
nationale de France.
Anna Tetas.
Velomax

Photo credits

Richard Copans p. 202 (video images)
Michel Denancé p. 20, 21, 24, 27, 32, 39, 44, 46, 50-51, 56, 57, 62, 66-67, 68-69, 100-101, 129, 146, 152 to 158, 161, 164, 232 to 238, 254, 256, 328, 331
Georges Fessy p. 94, 102, 103, 110-111, 113, 115, 120, 121, 124-125, 128, 133 to 141, 169, 170, 171, 180, 189, 193 to 196, 208 to 216, 222, 225, 242 to 248-249, 264 to 284, 296, 299, 303 to 322
Werner Huthmacher p. 340, 348-349, 353, 371, 376-377
IGN p. 168
Gaëlle Lauriot-Prévost p. 198, 201, 204, 206-207, 257, 290b, 291
André Morin p. 286, 288-289, 290a, 302
OSB-Grahn p. 332 to 335
Erik-Jan Ouwerkerk p. 360-361
Perrault Projets p. 16, 29, 160, 166, 218, 220-221, 260, 263, 362-363
Piel p. 174-175
Ramon Prat p. 18-19, 25, 26, 30-31, 34-35, 36-37, 40-41, 43, 45, 48-49, 55, 70 to 93, 98-99, 112, 114, 116 to 119, 122-123, 126, 127, 130-131, 336 to 339, 341 to 347, 352, 354 to 357, 370, 372 to 375
Giovanni Zanzi p. 182-183, 184-185, 192

Cover photograph:
Georges Fessy

This book was published on the occasion of the exhibition
Dominique Perrault,
Arquitecto Urbanista
organized by the Spanish Ministry
of Public Works and Urbanism in
Madrid, in February-March 1999.

This book is also available in a
French language edition
(ISBN 3-7643-6061-5).

A CIP catalogue record for this
book is available from the Library
of Congress, Washington D.C.,
USA

Deutsche Bibliothek Cataloging-
in-Publication Data
Perrault, Dominique:
Dominique Perrault, architect /
[transl.: Paul Hammond ...]. -
Basel ; Boston ; Berlin :
Birkhäuser, 1999
Franz. Ausg. u.d.T.: Perrault,
Dominique: Dominique Perrault,
architecte
ISBN 3-7643-5997-8 (Basel ...)
ISBN 0-8176-5997-8 (Boston)

Printed on acid-free paper
produced from chlorine-free pulp.
TCF∞
Printed in Spain
ISBN 3-7643-5997-8
ISBN 0-8176-5997-8

9 8 7 6 5 4 3 2 1

This is not a monograph, that science based on precise study of a subject, a life, a man. This is an author's – or authors' – book in which visions, words, images intersect with diverse and multifarious readings of contemporary architecture, since to speak of and describe this is also to speak of other architectures. This is not an autistic work which only gives an account of itself, through itself and for itself: this is the expression of an ethic which takes architecture to be a cultural fact that draws sustenance from things beyond its own academic field. This is a place where human experiences and aesthetic sensibilities are interwoven and blended in total freedom. Lastly, this is a shared pleasure destined to be shared, like that city we are endlessly building and which we always hope will be a good place to live in.   Dominique Perrault, February 1999

Frédéric Migayrou

Elementary dispositions Dominique Perrault's architecture is truly non-hierarchical; it avails itself of all the elements of an earlier architectonics and rearranges these according to a deliberately conceptual logic. A whole set of procedures, from the design to its realization, are thus overturned.

THE ARCHITECT SEIZES UPON ALL THE MOMENTS THAT MAKE UP THE SEQUENCES LEADING TO THE CONCEPTION AND REALIZATION OF A BUILDING – THE PROCESS, THAT IS – AND MAKES THE LASTING MATERIAL OF AN INTERVENTION FROM THEM.

Behind these skills, these decisions, the complex study and development of the idea, which define the architect as a creator, it is time itself that is undoubtedly the object of the architect's whole attention, his only preoccupation, the permanent restlessness of a present he tirelessly seeks to actualize. Indeed, what Perrault's architecture challenges is the idea of time that has formed the very essence of architectural culture, an idea which turns every building into a monument, a memory, an idea which founds, which historicizes, which would like architecture to possess an historical rationale, a truth. Dominique Perrault pleads for validity in architecture, he wants architecture to be effective, to be experienced by all, to have an instant rapport with each of us. It is Enlightenment reason he attacks, a reason that has fueled classicalism, and modernism too, a reason that seeks after rules and laws, a reason that seeks to determine the principles which legitimate and control architectural form. Dominique Perrault derives his main principles from praxis, from an ongoing research in which he endlessly reinvents the specificity of a space, of a form, of an intervention. For him, architecture is a constantly renewed activity, a consistently original act, a set of decisions which organize a singular, unique situation. Architecture is no longer the result of a composition, but of a state of mind which calls equally on forms, materials and the abilities of all who participate in the elaboration of a project.

This implies, then, an architecture lacking in reference; neither modern, nor postmodern, it functions with urgency, is immediate in nature and rejects history. It would therefore be illusory, when grasping, when trying to define Perrault's work, to seek models or analogies drawn from superficial comparison. Certain objects are

Philosopher and art and architecture critic, he is Art Advisor to the French Ministry of Culture and to the architectural collection of the FRAC Centre. He has published *Jeff Wall, Simple Indication*, ed. La Lettre Volée, and *Bloc, le Monolithe Fracturé*, ed. HYX, as well as many articles on the work of Diller and Scofidio, M. Saee, Asymptote, Morphosis, Daniel Libeskind, Steven Holl...

present, but one can no longer speak of forms, and the cubes and parallelepipeds common in much of his work are only a priori devices; they are the outcome of transitory conventions, differing states of stabilization, of the management of a permanently mutating situation. Given its lack of syntax, of obvious linguistic elements, we cannot easily scrutinize his architecture for principles or referential images, such as a particular 'Miesian' use of glass, certain spatial organizations borrowed from Louis I. Kahn, which critics must have been quick to point to. Architectural culture does not possess here ineluctable authority, it has no set method; instead it is a material, a resource, a tool like any other. Dominique Perrault insists on an architecture without style, without expression, which does not entail definition, the precedence of any language. His work does not respond to a constant syntax, applicable according to the appropriateness of the situation, the program; it is not organized as an aesthetic project which holds knowledge, norms, a morality of practice in check. The project's definition is a direct consequence of the context, of the determining factors present in it, which are analysed, put forward as a resource, a particular richness which must be interpreted by means of the tools of architecture, and thus transfigured, reconverted.

FOR HIM, CONTEXT MEANS, LITERALLY, "WITH THE TEXT" — TO SUPPLEMENT WHAT ALREADY APPEARS TO MAKE SENSE, OR TO REVEAL WHAT IS NOT IMMEDIATELY LEGIBLE, THE LINES OF FORCE OF A LANDSCAPE BARELY PERCEPTIBLE ON AN OPEN EXPANSE OF GROUND OR IN A DESTRUCTURED ENVIRONMENT, SPATIAL ORGANIZATIONS THAT MUST BE REVALUED.

Dominique Perrault's conceptualism is not historicist, he does not dwell on the memory of a place, of an extant building, he is tectonic, he takes physical hold of the territory. To dig beneath a small château to house the Usinor-Sacilor conference center (1991), and to place the château on a mirror surface that reflects back this architecture of representation, is to deny this arrogant play with inscription and representation that nourished 19th century architecture; it is to nullify the play of historical reference and to retain merely the slightly antiquated image of a building whose volume is exceeded by the program it now hosts. The traditional diagnosis of usage and function is only one of the aspects of the work, which is henceforth also built around an environmental analysis of defined or defining areas. The sum of elements which define and organize the specificity of a site – its history, social usage, its topography – are assimilated to a force-field which, in order to optimize its use and management, the architect addresses in its entirety. The lines of force organizing the territory are defined in this way, as is splendidly demonstrated in the model for the redevelopment of the Île Sainte-Anne in Nantes (1994), in which raw materials applied to an aerial view of the site generate lines of tension, vectors and zones capable of articulating and redefining the economy of this particular territory. In opposition to a sociological reading which looks for traces of the sedimentation of human praxis in the city or the territory, Perrault strives to be a geographer or a geologist; he rejects the authority of a past age, of an external time, of history, and retains only its current, active elements. Space does not possess its own ontology; for Perrault there is no antecedent, essence or primary nature which would rule over the built domain and which would have to be opposed to human praxis. There are, argues Perrault, "different natures," extending from the most virgin to the most artificial, natures which coexist in a simultaneous whole. This materialism, this veritable physicalism, redefines the world as a complexity in which man rediscovers his capacity for definition, for intervention.

NATURE IS NO LONGER THE DOMAIN OF INDETERMINACY, SHE ASSERTS HERSELF AS AN OBJECT OF KNOWLEDGE, SHE IS SUBMITTED TO THE LAWS OF REGULATION AND INDUSTRIAL PRODUCTION, SHE IS EXPLOITED, EXHAUSTED IN THE EXTREME, BUT SHE IS ALSO AVAILABLE FOR MASTERING ANEW; NATURE CAN BE DEVELOPED, SHE IS THE OBJECT OF SPECIFIC STUDY AND DEVELOPMENT.

To cultivate nature is to produce her, it is to avail ourselves of all the various kinds of knowledge we have at our disposal to induce her, to supplement her, to energetically endow her with a syntactical potential that is central to architectural language. And so Perrault conceives a hanging-garden-like forest for the International Port

Terminal in Yokohama (1994); he makes the Kansai-Kan Library disappear into the earth of a landscaped park; and of course he inscribes an inaccessible pine forest at the center of the Bibliothèque nationale de France in Paris (1989-95). Behind the apparent violence or arbitrariness of these interventions, an actual mutation in the relationship between nature and architecture articulates the logic of design. If vegetation has long been the object of human engineering – a fiction of natural order within the classical garden – the idea of the park, the forest, requires from the architect of today to call on all the technical dimensions of an understanding of the environment in order to go beyond the still-formalist logics of landscapism. When Dominique Perrault proposes such a brutalist use of nature, he does so to allow its phenomenal and sentient force to freely express itself, contra any overly cultural or architectural understanding of the garden, of green space. It is the landscape as a whole which is under scrutiny, which is saved from the endless temptations of planning. Architecture must not take possession of space; it no longer defines the measure of a geometric order. Instead, it must use every means at its disposal to remain aloof from spatial hierarchies and to yield to the possibilities of simultaneous action. The architect must, according to Dominique Perrault, generate the effects of spatiality; he must, by using simple gestures, create an order which rejects all mediation, a unique and immediate layout which does not strive to be a system, an organizing principle. Space must be concretely apprehended, brought into being according to a factual system, a unique, open-ended experience. Architecture must stick to this economy of layout in which space is defined through the sort of simple intervention Dominique Perrault has endlessly proposed: incrusting, weaving, enclosing, engraving, installing, anchoring, sectioning, blending, splicing, extending, flooding, concealing.

Is there a Dominique Perrault minimalism? Can we really define a minimalist architectural aesthetic long after the critical success of this art movement in the USA? The analytical contrivances of a spatial definition based on the disposition of primary elements, as seen in the works of a Walter de Maria or Richard Long, are widely deployed in many projects in order to attain an urban scale. The architectural object is reaffirmed as an element that gives space a direction, as a vector that renders the spectator conscious of a space which once seemed transparent to him, unquestioned evidence of the wide expanse. The building-as-object is reduced to a function by which it is all but refuted; it is a device of disposition, it is generic to an actualization of the site. This reduction is not, however, the effect of a kind of purism or of a simple economy of means aimed at reducing architectural language, analogous to Mies van der Rohe's famous "less is more." Space is no longer just this simple possibility, the final, modern form of Miesian space organized, as Beatriz Colomina once noted, by a gaze turned towards a horizon completely permeated by transparency. In contradistinction to the modern space of the tabula rasa, there is no spatial precedence, no pure, virgin space, no infinite white expanse – minimalism for Perrault means that there is no a priori, given space.

MINIMALISM, HERE, DOES NOT STAND FOR A REDUCTION OF MEANS, BUT RATHER AN AMPLIFICATION OF MEANS THAT HAVE THEIR STARTING POINT IN A REDUCED SYNTAX.

Any project will begin with a pragmatic investigation into how to understand the territory, and the layout of elements forming a spatial field will lead, as often happens in the case of Carl Andre, to a displacement of spatial tension. The architect tries to induce a physicality which has to be experienced by simultaneously appealing to an individual perception that has constitutional value and, more universally, to urban scale. It is the active dimension of this minimalist perspective which will dominate an architecture that appears, more and more, like an architecture having its legitimation in the intervention. Circle and square, the Berlin velodrome and Olympic swimming pool (1992-98) give material form to these combined investigations in which layout is ordained as a principle, the intersection of an idea and a location, the moment when concept and context coincide, as Dominique Perrault himself put it (Exhibition at the Galerie Denise René, 1991). Struts that cross each other and brace a walkway guide the design for the Charles de Gaulle Bridge (1988). A sheet of lead tied to a surface becomes an allegory of the relationship between the building and the ground it is on. An object-concept, the conception of an object, the layout frees architecture from the design, the plan; it organizes the territory in an order born of practice, of shared experience. The plan is not a previously defined field, and this once more calls into question a practice of spatial organization and the architectural vocabulary it supports: distribution, composition, hierarchization... The notion of plan leads to the idea of a potential inscription which is itself accompanied by words like insertion, limit, foundation, opening — words which denote an almost ideological vision of surface. Architecture is, in fact, an art of separation. It delimits, circumscribes, raises walls which define and constrain the architectural object. If Mies van der Rohe fulfilled the very idea of separation by transfiguring it into a wall of glass, Perrault goes as far as to deny the very idea of the window; a refusal of the idea of opening as a compositional element, in which the relationship between inside and outside is rejected. Not the least of the paradoxes of this so-called minimal architecture is to invert the logic of the curtain-wall, to repudiate a metaphysics of separation which still claims absolute transparency. The entire syntax of a relationship to the plan, the surface, implodes, then, beneath the blows of this open logic of layout. The wall is therefore rejected in favor of the enclosure, the medieval square plan of the Bibliothèque nationale de France (1989-95), the suspended structures of the Wilhelmgalerie (1993), the design of the Grande Stade in Melun-Sénart (1993).

The arbitrary enclosure, a squaring of the design, freed from the constraints of the economy of the plan, creates an incredible feeling of openness. The ground is no longer an obstacle, a frontier, a limit in itself; it is part of the program and is no longer left as the mere underpinning of the foundations. Dominique Perrault does not hesitate to involve it in the majority of his projects (the Angers Université de lettres et de droit, 1986), to merge the built object into the ground, leaving only a trace of it on the surface, like the almost graphic stigmata of the circle and square of the Berlin velodrome and swimming pool. As the Hôtel Industriel Jean-Baptiste Berlier (1986-91) shows, the floors are storage shelves on which men or objects are placed, on which different functional elements are moved around, and which no longer refer to a particular level, to a functional hierarchy.

Without walls the box has a merely conventional value, it is an enclosure, it protects a territory, it forms a refuge; it is also an enceinte which, protected by an envelope which permanently gives onto the world, has an almost matrical function.

This rejection of dividing walls gives rise to a new kind of curtain, a veiling materialized in the insistent use of metal mesh, or by means of the effective transparency of a sheet of glass, rapidly concealed by a second screen layer. Again paradoxically, Dominique Perrault insists on the use of grids which, liberated from the plan, from the control of perspectival projections, become a conventional device, a simple pattern that no longer refers to the idea of an external spatial continuum. The grid creates a regular area which can be articulated on top of another; it is merely the layout tool, it is a moment's activity, an affirmation that is, of course, subject to scrutiny, to change, to distortion, to making way for some other kind of organizing principle. Façades, floors, partitions – the grid is an ineludible syntactic element in Dominique Perrault's work, which for all that has no structural value; it remains a raw element exactly like the material itself, it has just as much formal as material value. The actual status of the materials must change, they no longer have syntactic value in their own right, along the lines of glass or brick. The material is form and matter at one and the same time, wood, greenery, metal mesh; it attains a specific qualifying potential, it is valued for its phenomenality, be it raw matter or industrial texture. The whole hierarchy of construction is overturned, procedures and usages becoming interchangeable. Nature is an object of engineering that can be chosen at will among endless possibilities, in order, perhaps, to render her effects more natural. High-precision technological materials can equally as well be used for their symbolic charge, for the phenomenal and emotional effect they convey. Vegetation granted object-status; industrial materials will be instead naturalized to the extreme. A phenomenon of general translatability, nature and the industrial world interpenetrate, everything is legible in terms of accumulated procedures, of serviceability, nothing is frightening any more, there are no more deprived areas, peripheries, wastelands, there is only a state of things. Dominique Perrault takes the idea of flexibility to its limit by assuming the world of industrial production to be a physical domain.

In a word, Perrault's oeuvre is without style, without expression, it does not encumber itself with any affectation, any code or presupposed knowledge. It invites a sort of unknowing, a refusal of any supposed meaning, of architecture as a defining principle. Dominique Perrault runs the idea of a meaning in architecture to ground; within a very French tradition, he argues for the boundaries of a metaphysics in which architecture must accept the principle of its own disappearance. The gesture is not new; the end of humankind, the end of philosophy, the end of history — years ago structuralism had already made declarations of this kind familiar to us. What he dissimulates is the refusal of typologies, of a preexisting language that could be applied to any definition of space. His minimalism does not lead to the phenomenal truth of a purer space being elaborated from a new purism which balances light and materials. Perrault's architecture strikes at the very heart of a structuralist vision of creation which presupposed the permanent equivalence, traducible in linguistic terms of the means the architect has, a syntactic understanding that had swamped all the debates between moderns and postmoderns in the tumultuous questioning of meaning and expression. Dominique Perrault dismisses this quest for architectural truth, this historicism of the postmoderns, this yielding to a phenomenology of modernism with its Heideggerian overtones, by challenging current appeals to certain principles of authority. There is no subjectivism remaining in the background any more, no subject of history or of expression, be that subject collective or individual; architecture can no longer maintain its authority through intentional distance. Turning to Maurice Blanchot, Perrault speaks of blank writing, takes architecture beyond the traditional realms of expression. He confines himself to the founding event of an architectural "there is." This claim immediately takes on a political connotation, the end of the profession, of the architect; the discipline must be practised without distance, without limits, it resides in the displacements of identity between monumental and human, self-publicity and intimacy, between city and nature. "Nothing," the text in which Perrault attempts to rediscover a primary phenomenal meaning to architecture, and in which the body and emotion are established as modes of experiencing and understanding space, has not simply a passive dimension.

PERRAULT'S CONCEPTUALISM IS NO LONGER SIMPLY ANALYTICAL AND CRITICAL; IT HAS AN OPERATIVE FUNCTION, IT DEEMS DISPOSITION TO BE AN AUTHENTIC CONSTRUCTIVE PRINCIPLE. BY NEUTRALIZING ARCHITECTURE, DOMINIQUE PERRAULT INVENTS A PATH LEADING TO PROXIMITY IN THE ARCHITECT'S WORK, AN ARCHITECTURE IN ACT, A MANIFEST ARCHITECTURE OF THE NEUTRAL.

Hôtel Industriel Jean-Baptiste Berlier

ARCHITECTURE IS NOT AN ART OF EXCLUSION   Five years ago, in the 13th arrondissement, the City of Paris, together with the Société Anonyme de Gestion Immobilière, launched an urbanistic-architectural competition to try and see what could be done with "that bit of land" trapped between the Périphérique clover leaf, the Quai d'Ivry, and the bundle of tracks of the Gare d'Austerlitz.

As if the site did not leave it unaffected, the brief proposed, in its own way, the implementation of an abstraction, "an industrial HQ," a new type of building that was neither offices nor industrial premises, simply an "intelligent" space, housing occupants with a wide range of different activities whose evolution could not be foreseen: WHITE SQUARE ON WHITE BACKGROUND. Nothing, less than nothing, no footing, no hold, no hook, no soothing theories about the city with-parks-and-gardens, but a confrontation with "our world," the one out there, the real, so-called "tough" world, the one we pretend we don't want, the one we've come to terms with; in fact, a "softly-spoken" contemporary cityscape with road haulage depots, motorways, rubbish-incineration plants, a cement-manufacturer's silo, a helicopter pad for medical emergencies, a traffic control and maintenance center for the 250,000 vehicles a day driving on the Périphérique. Let's stop thinking about the existence of such BLIGHTED PLACES and absorb their energy instead, right where it's given off. Let's bring another vision to this ceaseless traffic of trundling, flying objects, the city's perpetual motion, and go on bringing to it a "certain something," a "je ne sais quoi" which, with "the best will in the world," will provide evidence of the place's transfiguration. Let's get on with it, then – plant ourselves bang in the middle of the site, in full view of this fantastic spectacle of urbanity. To get the most out of it, let's work, bathed in a natural light picked up by a GLASS BOX, surround ourselves with all kinds of services, comfort at all levels, networks, connections, in order to be able to adapt to changing ways of life and modes of production. Contained in this glass brick will be forty or so businesses employing five hundred people: some of these businesses will flourish, others disappear, the building will not remain indifferent to these changes, the evolution of its activities will always be visible up front, and that will be the expression of its reality.

To live happily, let's not live in hiding. It's not a question of constructing a historic building, an eco-museum on hold, but a living system vibrant with the shock-waves of its present environment, because this object is there, and not elsewhere. **DP, 1990**

Robert Kramer

Paris is old and composed and zipped up. But, out on the eastern edge of the city, the confusion and violence break free. That place breathes, it is raw, chaotic, the way it is everywhere in the States and for the same reasons, all the transitions are naked and exposed and pushed up against each other.

The Hôtel Industriel Berlier is right next to the Périphérique, the circular highway that encloses Paris. Open tracks feeding the Gare d'Austerlitz close Berlier in on its south side. Now it depends on which way you look. Huge silvery smokestacks of the garbage treatment plant, old warehouses, a flour mill, a wall of high-rise apartment blocks, the continuous flash of trains, a flow of cars, the Seine: a sense of the work that the city implies, of its system of needs, and the evolution of how these needs get grafted onto the body. It is a story of wild energy, of energy out of control, of capitalism and of violence. It is *industrial* in a 19th century way, and if you have that in you, then you understand when Perrault says that the most beautiful boulevard of Paris isn't the Champs Élysées, but the Péripherique.

Floor-to-ceiling windows, exposed air-cooling system, a metallic latticework that seems to package the glass structure (and which functions as a *brise-soleil*): the Hôtel Industriel Berlier is a transparent structure, made to let the energy of the place flow into it. The functional exo-skeleton joins with the steel bands of train tracks, the signal towers and the Périphérique itself. Berlier is just another element in that collage of structures. It is as incongruous as all the other elements, and together they make a compact mass of contradictions, an image that has the character of a city's backdoor. The redevelopment of this part of the 13th *arrondisement* involved the destruction of a traditional site of small-scale business, manufacturing and crafts. Berlier was commissioned by the city of Paris to provide affordable alternative space, in an effort to keep these small proprietors within the city limits. The interior design reflects this. Floor space is there to be divided up, depending on the needs of the renters. And the variety of renters corresponds to the variety outside the glass walls. A homeopathic laboratory, woodworking, printing, hi-tech furniture, Chinese fabric workers, polystyrene molding, Perrault's own offices, a photo agency, a workshop providing jobs for the disabled. Something here about an open, modular space divided up in many different ways, large ethnic diversity, different levels of technology and styles of work, different classes of workers, a kind of *souk* in a glass cube, hanging over a highway at the edge of the city.

Film director born in New York City. He has lived and filmed abroad for the past 20 years. Recently, he was surprised to discover that he had paid too little attention to contemporary architecture as a primary expression of the actual relations of power, and therefore of the inherent limits of the possible. This carelessness is especially flagrant in view of the fact that he has been filming these very towers and towns, these stage sets of an official narrative, for over 35 years.

Up the elevators, through the corridors, you don't feel this aspect much: perhaps a little, in the variety of people you pass. But passing Berlier from the Périphérique what you see are all the things that have been laid and stacked against the windows. After all, these windows are the walls of the workshops, and the random collage of things arranged or merely placed and forgotten, are the signs of a spectacularly chaotic human capacity to occupy a space in whatever ways possible. The *kitsch* of the window is a sign of the variety within. This pasting things up on the windows (perhaps also to get some more shade), the open shelves, the need to store things wherever they can go, only underlines the feel of this building as an arbitrary enclosure of a certain volume of that immensely energetic space.

The center of this story, however, is violence. The embracing of the totalized violence our civilization has created, a celebration of that violence as pure energy, and a certain willful, virile pleasure in being capable of adapting to it. A Darwinian joy, a thrill of power. I think the very transparency of the Berlier has something to do with Dominique Perrault's own desire to be present in this world as it is. To fight there, with those tools, on that turf: to be a contender in that harsh cityscape. Which is what Dominique sees when he sits at his desk, looking out as far as the eye can see through the glass wall beyond the desk and telephones.

I've been in that building a few long afternoons and evenings, there to film, waiting for the last light. The sounds of the air-cooling system, the traffic below, the trains, bleed into a sound of surf or breathing. Watery, flow and flux and flood, transience, and the flash of cars passing below is hypnotic; they seem to go into the building itself and out the other side, abstract particles, cells pumping through an artery. And rising from the incineration plant, smoke masses in the darkening sky, huge amoeba forms made solid by the angle of the dropping sun.

And at last, it's very melancholy, all this — the rush of watery sound, the constant movement with no other reason that its own moving. Melancholy and remote.

And to the west, now looking into the setting sun, there stand the giant slabs of the Bibliothèque Nationale, black rectangles against the low sun behind them: markers, signs, like Pharaonic tombstones or monoliths from some fabulous contemporary Stonehenge, rising up through the dusky redness that obscures all the detail of the city. Melancholy and desolate, because all the words are there, all the books that describe how we got there.

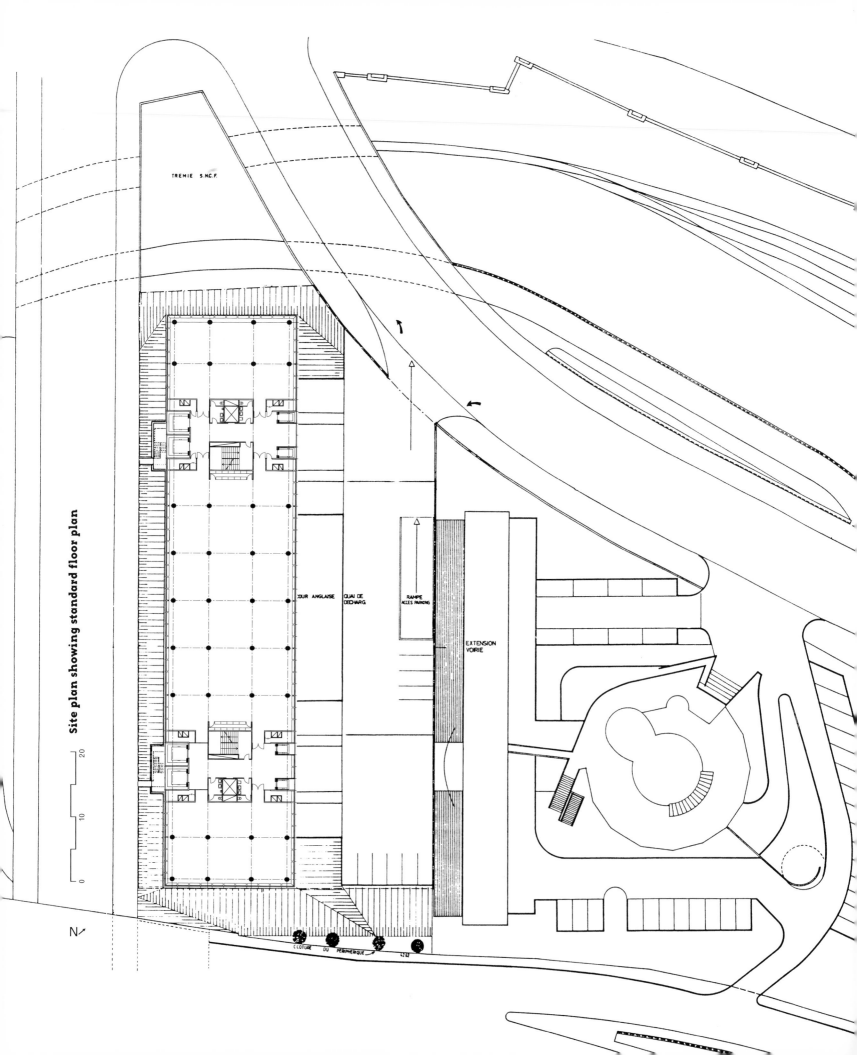

Site plan showing standard floor plan

TREMIE S.N.C.F.

COUR ANGLAISE QUAI DE DECHARG.

RAMPE ACCES PARKING

EXTENSION VOIRIE

CLOTURE DU PERIPHERIQUE

N

20

10

0

Water treatment plant SAGEP

Ivry-sur-Seine, 1987-1993

Odile Fillion What is a water treatment plant if not a vast machine consisting of gigantic pumps, sophisticated networks of sluices, filters, wide pipes, cisterns, stretches of water, of miles of catwalks? A machine, however, can be a work of architecture. It is in this context that Dominique Perrault was invited in 1989 to plan the renovation and extension of a water treatment plant, a program which is still mainly the job of the engineer. It was more a question, then, of "sheathing" than of designing.

Apart from a 200-meter strip next to Ivry, the other workings of this 9-hectare plant by the Seine are strictly invisible and closed to the public. A priori, the compact of the plant's architectural image is therefore minor, and has more to do with thinking about an interior landscape, with offering optimal working conditions.

In the first instance, the project involves the plant's *mise en scène* using color and light, spread over all the site's technical systems. Only a slim laboratory and office building, placed on pilotis at the center of the site and whose aluminum façade is punctuated by a set of random horizontal openings, alludes in a more classical way to architecture. Perhaps the most spectacular in this series of interventions is the idea of a peripheral cowling, like a rectangular and transparent giant buoy, 8 meters tall. This glass and metal cylinder now forms the frontage of the plant facing the town. Behind the glazed curves, the technical equipment of a maintenance gallery, an architect's idea for "rescuing" the personnel from the damp workings under ground.

Journalist, specialized in the production of videos on contemporary architecture. she was awarded the Prix de la promotion architecturale (mention) in 1990. Former co-editor of *Le Moniteur* (1988-1994), editor in chief of *Archi-cree* (1982-1988) and *L'écho des caue* (1976-1981). She currently conducts a radio weekly program on architectural criticism on France Culture.

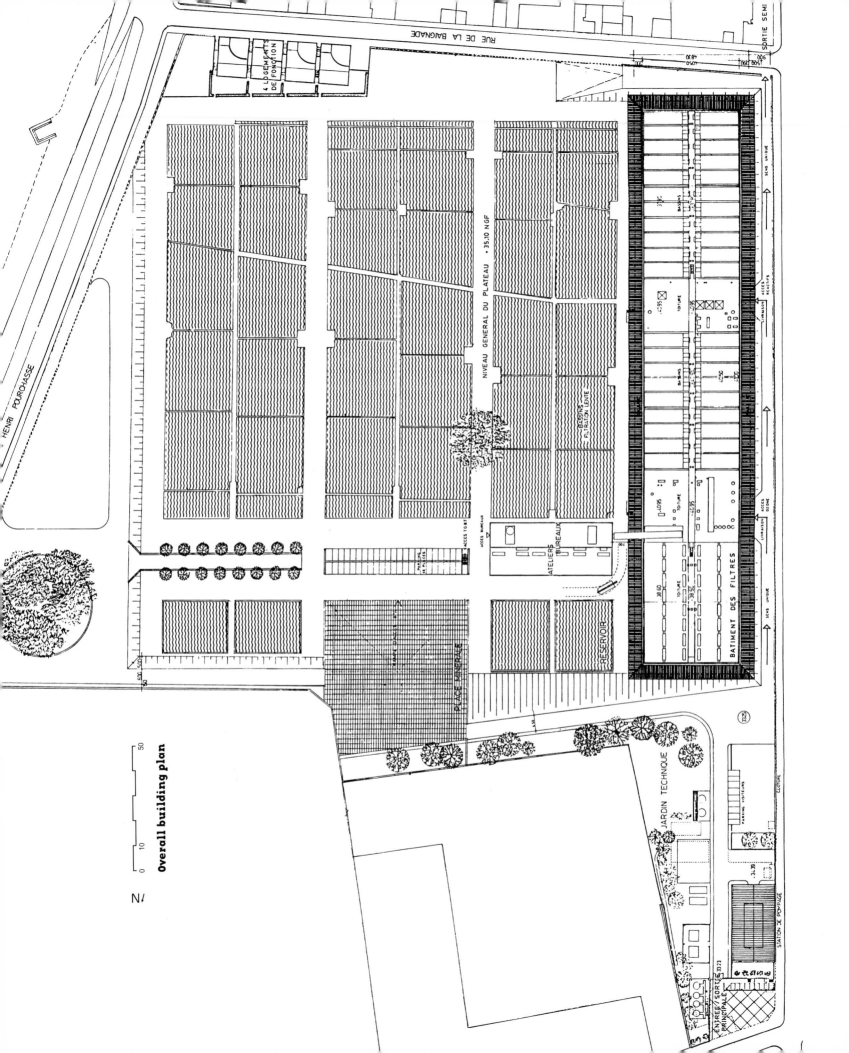

Overall building plan

IRSID
USINOR-SACILOR
Conference Center

Saint-Germain-en-Laye, 1989-1991

Vis-à-vis the charm of the château and of its "jewel-case of green," the addition or attachment of a new building seems contradictory, complicated and unsightly. In fact, what is called for is the revaluation and restoration of the existing building. In placing the château "on a glass plate" one creates a conspicuous place and a clearly-defined marker.

This conspicuousness results from the tactful insertion of the new extension which incorporates the lower part of the château into a glass volume which is set into the ground. The geometry of this circular-shape base draws to it the many approaches that follow the main axis, the future entrance and even the walkways at the far end of the park.

The glass disk filters the natural light and plays with the artificial light. This plate will, in effect, be smooth and shiny by day. The château will be reflected in it, as in a stretch of water. At nightfall, however, the effect will be the opposite, because the surface will be lit up, illuminating the château.

You could describe this project as a "glass and steel device," the reactions to which testify to the vitality of the building qua object, as well as to that of the surroundings.

The spatial organization of the different functions is divided between "spaces for meetings," located in the château, and "spaces for communication," situated in the base. The whole thing is linked together by a stairway set at the center of the device.

The communications center is accessed through the château via a metal footbridge extending over the glass disk.

Seen in plan, a concentric system extends around the ancient building. In the central part, an area for services and corridors is located beneath the château, then a crown which integrates the restaurant and auditorium, and finally a technical ring grouping the service entrances and emergency exits. **DP, 1989**

Hitchcock/Perrault   Richard Copans

Foreword   If this were a child's game, it would be a drawing. The drawing of a landscape in which you have to recognize, hidden in the foliage, at the reverse of the landscape or in a cloud, the shape of an animal or a face. A game of observation: the sign which enables the hidden meaning of the drawing to be unlocked is hidden in the corners of the same drawing. Here, in this park with its ancient trees, we may be caught by the same childlike interrogation; in this landscape there is some architecture, and recent architecture at that. Before understanding, loving or rejecting it, you first have to find it... It's difficult, though, to turn the landscape upside-down, like the child does with the drawing that intrigues him. Is it between the willow, the cedar and the chestnuts? Where the hell has Dominique Perrault hidden his architecture?

Hitchcock   The bourgeois house that sits in the middle of the park is probably around a hundred years old. Not really a château, nor a hunting lodge, but an elegant home for a wealthy family not far from the forest of Saint-Germain-en-Laye. A few bas-reliefs with little chubby angels decorate the bottoms of the windows; and the balcony ledges use cement to imitate wood. Misfortune must have hit the family. Maybe the kids squabbled over the inheritance, or one of them gambled it all away, or... The family house has become the "Château d'Usinor" outside Paris. It isn't really menacing, this house... Just a little, like those traces of the past which you invest with former dramas, long-dead times. It resembles a bit, a tiny bit (just enough to...), that old California baroque house, the main set in Hitchcock's *Psycho*. The comparison could end there. But a profound link unites the two buildings.

The Crime   In the two houses a crime has been committed. In the two houses the crime was committed in identical circumstances: ...under water...
In the motel run by Anthony Perkins (alias Norman Bates), Janet Leigh dies from repeated blows of a knife under a boiling hot shower. In the Château d'Usinor, the architecture is sunk beneath a tranquil lake.
In Saint-Germain-en-Laye, no strident Bernard Hermann music;
the wind in the trees is the only music.
And the perfect round of a virtual lake beneath which Perrault has sunk the

Filmmaker and producer of both documentaries and feature films. He founded Films d'Ici in 1984, has directed since 1992, together with Stan Neumann, the series "Architectures" on Arte, and since 1998 the series "Les mots de l'architecte" on Paris Première.

Conference Center the client requested. A lake of glass encircles the little château. A moat that encircles, protects and reflects the building. A perfect screen for separating past from present and permitting them different kinds of mirror-play, whatever the time of day or night.

"What is it that is stronger than water?" (a 14th century Chinese riddle)

Answer: the idea of water.

The proof: you need a footbridge to reach the château, a footbridge which soars, delicately, above the glass surface.

Frozen time The glass surface prevents any contamination between epochs. It separates, sections, slices up time.

May the trace of the past linger on, right where it is, among the trees... The future is above ground-level, materially inscribed below the horizon line. The present is that thin layer of glass we are walking on.

We can now traverse history, come and go freely through the heights and the depths of the building. Traverse different epochs, no problem. And the lift attendant (if there was one) might announce:

Ground Floor: Present, Entrance, please wipe your feet

Basement: Future, Conference Center, the future is radiant (yet hidden).

Take in the wind in the trees and mind that the past doesn't weigh you down!

First and Second Floor: Past, study rooms, see the tops of the trees, and if you lean out, you'll see the future. To exit, take the stairs!

The Territory At the end of the tree-lined avenue, behind the ornate railings, the same château. Same foliage, same seasonal colors all around. A single new sign, as if placed on the ground: a gleaming disk reflecting the sky and all its changes.

A sign on the ground and everything's turned inside-out.

By Way of a Conclusion: From Hitchcock to Cocteau

Norman Bates (who identifies himself with the mother he's killed and who sometimes takes over from her with dress, chignon and knife) says: "Mother, I have to take you down to the cellar because they'll be coming to watch us."

Dominique Perrault addresses the same words to Architecture – mother-of-all-the-arts. And rejoins Cocteau telling the mirrors to "get on with reflecting..."

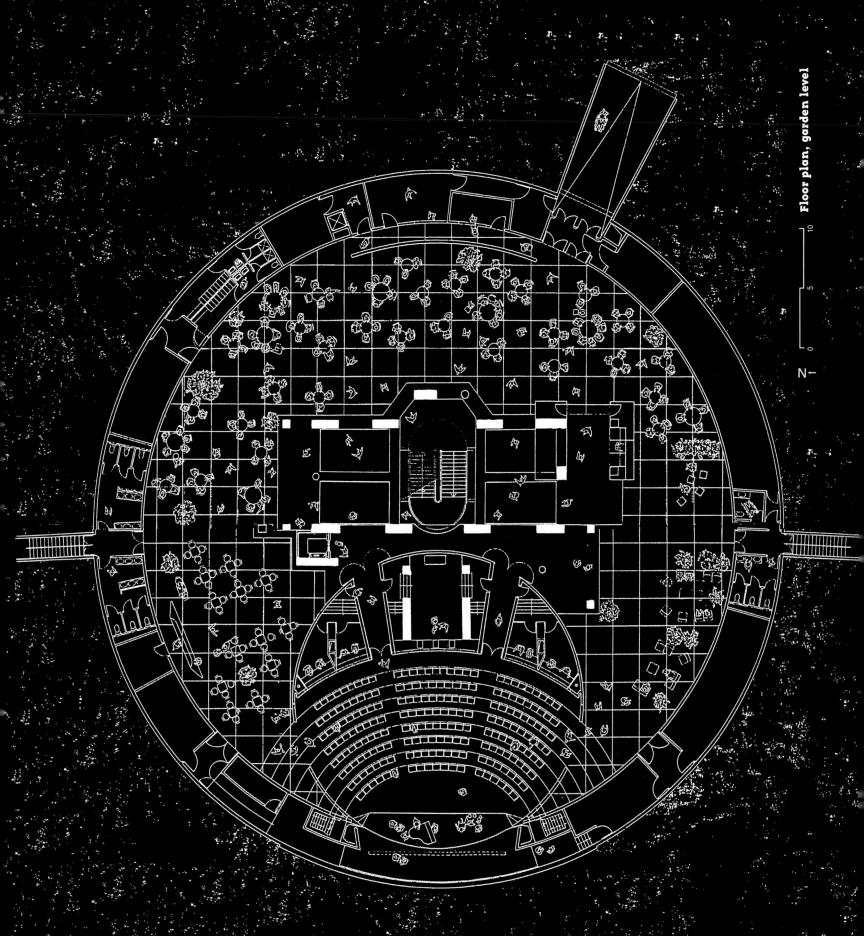

N

THE ARCHITECT WITHIN HIS CONTEXT

What is this profession, this work of intervention, this action on what is usually called a landscape, this whole made up of natural elements, of architecture, of networks...? We like this form of accumulation, this complexity of the landscape – it implies a real relationship based on acceptance, the understanding of a situation, of a context, whatever it be. If we consider that the places we may encounter are not predetermined by fate, that nothing is fixed forever, then intervention is always possible. Fate is determinant if there is no longer life, if there is no evolution or possibility of modifying a site. But to the extent that there is awareness, a need, an interest, a desire for modification, for transformation, transfiguration even, at that moment there is no more fate, there is action, creation. How do we designate what follows, that action?

Work is a highly polymorphous affirmation; it involves a great many elements, assumes extremely varied forms which may extend from a reinforcement or an exaggeration of presence to almost total disappearance. This prior accumulation does not disturb us, does not handicap us; on the contrary, it interests us. It is not an acceptance in the historicist sense, the taking into account of a socio-historical domain, but an acceptance in the geographical sense.

...is fact constitutes a tremendous break as far as the analytical perception of a ...ace is concerned. It is nonetheless necessary to take history into account, but as ...ne factor among all the others, and what is decisive in this history is that it has ...roduced a certain type of geography. To have a criteria of taste, to think in ...esthetic terms, to judge in qualitative terms are not prerequisites for intervention ...a site. That would be to enter into an area of judgement in which we partly evade ...e essential energy of the place, keeping to the position of a spectator, an analyst ...r critic who wants to keep his distance. Work should be much more physical, ...ore intuitive, during the encounter with this environment. It is a confrontation, ...e telescoping of a gaze and a place. The diagnosis is not the result of pure ...nalytical effort, but of an encounter that does or does not happen.

...aced with a site, my first idea is not to change things. Contrary to the architect, ...have no vision in mind, the encephalogram line remains absolutely straight. ...n the other hand, I am approached with a question, a request that is different. ...t that moment there is a project, because there is a demand that is beyond the ...xternal will of the architect. In fact, the preliminary experience of the site, ...he place, crowds the mind, and to rid yourself of that vision can take a lot of time. ...ut if it is stipulated that what is involved is a national library within a European ...ontext, a European capital, a stretch of industrial wasteland beside a river flowing ...hrough a capital city, that suffices to start us thinking without having seen anything ...eginning with these extremely generic elements, a space of reflection, of ...ormulation, is created. This first critical definition sets a frame for the confrontation ...f the real situation and structures a kind of interactivity with the context which ...reserves a distant view of things. If we immediately go and look at the site, it gets ...n the way, disturbs us, it blocks the work to a certain point. The academic idea of ...iagnosis bears the mark of a certain complacency. For me, the architect does not ...egulate, does not recommend a therapy. Behind this seemingly ultra-provocative ...ay of reasoning, this refusal to see the site, to be contaminated by the factual and this notion of context ought to be established. Such prior reflection is not, for all that, abstract; it merits recognition as an applied work undertaken in a phase which is already operational. The transformation of a site requires a dialog we have to prepare ourselves for. In the first instance, everything is defined according to a kind of feeling towards the place, the idea we may have of it, and the actual confrontation with reality. It is a rather violent relation, short on indulgence, to which we must bring something if we want to be part of it. This relationship with reality means that things assume a certain place, which, without being definitive, allows us to position various elements of dialog and analysis in place, and thus to finally structure the demands and define the relationship with the building process. In the case of the Bibliothèque nationale de France, the image of a world-famous historical monument came to mind, with its central volume and its minarets. The elimination of the main volume led to an extremely forceful idea which left monumentality in a state of indecision, of hesitation between absence, the trace of a past and a future, the anticipation of a possible complementary construction – something which exists without being there. This is an example of the creation of a set of conditions to encounter a place. An open attitude, a certain form of freedom have to be recreated.

Intervention is more a phenomenon of inclusion than of exclusion. It is an approach that is based on the use of the more or less distinctly felt energy of a place in order to give it greater presence, further resonance, to amplify it.

In the case of the site of the Hôtel Industriel Jean-Baptiste Berlier, we think it is more the mass that is going to lend presence to the architectural object in relation to an environment crossed by flows and movements of enormous force and impact. Paradoxically, the building, with its effect of mass, will remain light and airy, even though traversed by the various systems that are visible through the glass façades, which assimilate it even better to the environment. The understanding of the context is thus neither formalist nor spatial, nor uniquely historical. When faced with the interventions of artists like Richard Long or Walter de Maria in a gallery or an open space, we understand that, according to the simple disposition of elements, an order seems to emerge. The installation of a metal piece will completely transfigure our understanding of a space. The actual alignments of stones or metal objects, implicated in vast environments lends enormous resonance to wild and natural landscapes. If architecture exists, it is right there, in events like these that define the true power of architecture, according to that capacity the installation has, through a simple act, of transforming one environment into another, of strongly modifying our perception of the location. Land Art, minimalism and conceptual art displace our perception of space towards that relational dimension in which the object is no longer autonomous and loses its privileged identity.

On an urban scale it is not so much the form of the element, building or texture introduced that has importance, it is the positioning of this object in relation to an exterior configuration.

This means working on the relationship between things more than on the things themselves, working on the tension, on a set of interactions that is neither wholly spatial nor geometric. DP, 1998

Bibliothèque nationale de France

Paris, 1989-1995

A PLACE AND NOT A BUILDING   The *grands projets* of the President of the Republic François Mitterrand are all closely associated with a site, and a history – in short, a place with a name. The Bibliothèque nationale de France is to be built on a stretch of industrial waste land on the banks of the Seine in the East End of Paris. It represents the starting-point for a complete restructuring of this entire sector of the 13th arrondissement. The institution encompasses within it an element of Grandeur and an element of Generosity. If we refer ourselves to the urban history of the great monuments which have been fundamental signs of the city's thrust toward new territory, the greatest gift that it is possible to give to Paris consists, today, in offering space, and emptiness – a place that is open, free, and stirring. Accordingly, the enormous building, envisaged as a demonstration of architectural emphasis and affectation, is transformed into a piece of work on the void – an absolute luxury in the city – proposing to the History of France a focus on immateriality and non-ostentation. It is this context which engenders the concept of the project.

A SQUARE FOR PARIS   A Library for France. An initiatory place and not some monster of a building, part temple and part supermarket. A place of reference for the East End of Paris. A place that is part and parcel of the continuity of the sequence of large empty spaces along the Seine, like the Place de la Concorde, the Champ de Mars, and the Invalides. In this way, the site beside the Seine becomes one of major importance with the activation of this place. In an operation designed to save and redeem the place, the institution introduces its generosity, while the Bibliothèque nationale de France contributes its influence and radiance. With this combination of a free and open space, built to the scale of the capital, and horizontality, the Bibliothèque nationale de France unfurls its breadth and volume by way of its four "beacon"-like markers, akin to tension-rods or braces for the flat area between them, offering a verticality that defines a virtual volume, which, in turn, crystallizes all the magic, presence and poetry of the complex.

A SYMBOLIC PLACE   With its four corner towers resembling four open books, all facing one another, and delimiting a symbolic place, the Bibliothèque nationale de France – a mythical place – imposes its presence and identity on the scale of the city by the adjustment of its four

63

corners. These urban landmarks develop and enhance the idea of the "book" with a random occupation of the towers, which present themselves like an accumulation of learning, of knowledge that is never complete, and of a slow but on-going process of sedimentation. Other complementary metaphors spring to mind, be it book-towers, or silos, or vast racks with countless shelves, or vertical labyrinths, and all these unambiguous images converge on a powerful identity of these architectural objects. The establishment of an open square underpins the notion of availability, as applied to treasure. It is the towers which have helped to situate and identify this treasure as cultural. The public space will offer a direct and natural physical contact between the sacred institution and the man in the street. The inclusion of an "inlaid," sunken garden rounds off the symbolic siting of the project, offering a quiet spot away from the fuss and bother of the city. Like a cloister, this tranquil, unruffled space will invite contemplation and a flowering of intellectual endeavour.

A MAGIC PLACE   This project is a piece of art, a minimalist installation, the "less is more" of emotion, where objects and the materials of which they are made count for nothing without the lights which transcend them.

Towers, case- or sheath-like structures of glass, with a double skin and sun filters which multiply the reflections and magnify the shadows: the absolute magic of the diffraction of light by means of these crystalline prisms.

Nature offset, with a garden where all you see is the foliage of the trees. "A sea of trees, a froth of leaves." In short, the soft protection of undergrowth, with its aromas and rustling sounds, reunions with oneself, and with another world. Night vision: the Bibliothèque nationale de France will be set in a halo of light, emanating from the garden and the service periphery. A diaphanous light will rise up through the interiors of the glass towers, culminating in four topmost points, which will shimmer like four lighthouse beacons. This liquid light will spread over the square, while the towers will be reflected in the Seine.

AN URBAN PLACE   What could be more urban and more public than a pedestrian square? The challenge of creating a void preserves the future of the district, while at the same time steering its development and offering conspicuous architectural requirements, such as can be learnt from the great squares of Paris. A square is a space that is lined or hemmed: a system of continuous structures – combining porches, covered walks, and a cornice height forming a skyline – delimits the public place. This setting acts as a backdrop, not a water-front foreground. It will accommodate diverse and varied architectural scripts, the sole rule being their shared role of accompanying, in their own right, the institution's urban influence. **DP, 1989**

Toyo Ito

Death of Form, Form of Death   Dominique Perrault's photomontage describing
the concept of the Bibliothèque de France depicts a monument to the dead.
The white rectangular courtyard domain in the center looks like a coffin buried
in the ground, and the towers at its four corners distinctively identify the sacred
boundary, a sanctuary for the dead.
Some Japanese Shinto shrines have no built sanctuary. The shrine is merely
signified by four posts of burnished logs. The approach has *torii* (gates) and
Kaguraden (a stage structure to offer song and dance to god) aligned to it along an
axis, but the inner shrine where the god descends is a vacant piece of ground.
The four logs that mark the threshold of the sanctuary are taken from trees grown
in the mountains, sawn down, burnished and ritually renewed every seven years.
In praying before this empty shrine, people would be immersed in serene
tranquility and, owing to the emptiness, attain a state of spiritual purity.
Roland Barthes in *The Empire of Signs* referred to Tokyo as a city that indeed has
a center, but a center that is hollow. The entire city is built around a forbidden
space, protected in rich verdure and moat – the literally invisible residence
of the Emperor.
The center of Perrault's library is a sunken garden. The ground is cut out in a
rectangle and greenery planted on an artificial topography. Invisible from the
street, the verdure seems unreal, a landscape afloat in fragments of memory.
In the competition text Perrault himself emphasizes that he is creating a place,
not a building. He states that the greatest gift that it is possible to offer to Paris today
is space and emptiness. It is not only to be an urban square where people gather,
but a silent and peaceful place where the dead can be prayed to.
However, what does the idea of "the dead" represent here? Is it the nation?
The enormous accumulation of reading materials, perhaps? Or could it be the
history of knowledge inscribed in the books? Whatever the answer, it appears
to be a place where the history of power and glory of a past era is to be mourned.
Since modernism, the spatial concept of a library has been the "architectural-
ization" of Academicism and of the social discipline of past ages. That is,

**He started his own studio Toyo Ito & Associates Architects in Tokyo in 1971. His latest works include the L Hall in Nagaoka,
the O Dome in Odate, and the Notsuharu Town Office. His design for a mediatheque in Sendai is now under construction.
He is honorary Professor at the University of North London.**

the schematic display of shelved books has been the formalized spatial structure for a visualization of intellectualism. Étienne-Louis Boullée's design for a library had a vaulted roof, a line of pillars holding the roof, and countless layers of books receiving light from above. And the vault, the pillars and the massed books all taper in a single direction. The library of the British Museum by Anthony Panizzi, on the other hand, is a diagrammatic representation of Jeremy Bentham's utilitarianism. A circular floor, roofed over by a dome, is surrounded by a wall of books, and the reading tables in a radial layout focus on a central point. A perfect model of sweeping observation is realized here. Both examples are practical solutions sought for proposing intellectualism as pleasure: an attempt, then, to formalize life's richness through books.

It is possible to identify a focused architectural formalization in Perrault's library as well. The thoroughness of its formalization is readily perceived when compared to other submissions at the competition stage. It is clear that a completely different architectural thinking is applied here to the solutions commonly deriving from the requirements of contemporary libraries, such as the definition of a pleasant environment for reading in, or creating an ideal space for preserving the books. His intention to confront extreme functionalism and democratic expression can be sensed.

On the other hand, Perrault's proposal might be construed as Minimalist. If we look at his wider production, it is true that his works are often reduced to the minimal. However, they are not in the same category as the architectural application of minimalism in contemporary art. It is, rather, a purified form of expression that may be identified with Classicism, such as that of Boullée or Panizzi. Yet, does the French nation today endorse its library as a form resonant with its own death, or is it a monument to the death of its own intellectualism?

The four L-shaped towers obviously represent books. Unlike the customary library organization, they emphasize verticality. They are skyscrapers of books. No matter how the sun illuminates them, the spaces are intended to have a transparent quality. And yet they are not spaces for people to linger in, but spaces whose only purpose is to be systematically filled with an immense amount of books.

How, I enjoy asking myself, would Le Corbusier have responded if he were to see the sunlit, airy space reserved solely for books? And people being left to consult them in a space underground?

No matter how anti-humanist it may seem, the "skyscrapers of books" are a new architectural form of display, and in that sense, the French nation's endorsement of Perrault's proposal is understandable. Nevertheless, when I first approached this building, I was struck by how much more modest the towers were from what I had imagined. A sense of steadfastness was expressed, more than an expression of pretentiousness. What I found there was not the harsh shimmering of glass and metal, but modest book towers whose amicable expression derived from the combination of glass and wood. Their gentleness and modesty seem further amplified by the layering of wood over the foundation stairs. When a monumental quality is required of architecture, it is common practice to bring in stone, and here too, most architects would undoubtedly have selected stone. Nevertheless, Perrault deliberately opted for a simple wooden deck.

His simple and modest choice of materials, i.e., detail design, are maintained throughout the interior. Even manufactured products like the metal mesh he often uses do not give off glaring reflections but have a solemn austerity, as if of oxidized silver. His selection of interior materials and of wood for the furnishings has no ostentious expensiveness, but the subtlety of expression that one finds in prefabricated plywood.

This extremely understated, austere expression may be assumed to be a matter of taste, but I see it as a reflected image of the architect's own personality. It overlaps with the nonchalant manner of his speech and the earnest image of the architect, which he displayed when he personally guided me through the architecture.

His way of speaking was a far cry from that of an architect who is talking about a project of such national importance.

Judging by this library, I take Dominique Perrault to be an architect with two conflicting sides. Perrault witnessing the death of Classicism in architecture for one; plus Perrault trying to express his deeply felt sensibility. People who experience this architecture are drawn in, willingly or not, to its hollow center, but are never left feeling hollow.

His Olympic velodrome and swimming pool in Berlin suggest something similar. The spaces where athletes compete are buried in the ground, just like the reading room of the library. Even though the velodrome's floorplan is a perfect circle, the roof that covers the space is not a dome but a flat, trussed space-frame. The flat roof is not for walking on, however. Although it is almost flush with the surrounding ground, the image is one of a disk that floats by itself. Shielded by metal mesh, the disk emits a dull light. It is simply there, unmoving. We are faced, here, with another funerary monument.

As a space to contain the excitement of what goes on inside, of sports competitions that call for the extreme speed of trained and drilled athletes, and the spectators' excitement as athletes strive to better records by one tenth of a second, one hundredth of a second, the interior of this arena may be too direct. The ceiling exposing the steel structure of the trusses seems like the interior of a factory, and is devoid of all relation to the exaltation of the activities within. Once again, Perrault's earnest and straightforward way of expressing himself can be sensed throughout. Here, the excitement and frenzied atmosphere are tightly enclosed within the disk.

For Perrault, practicing architecture is probably a process of seeking confirmation of the death of architectural formalism. Many 20th century architects have relished the freedom granted by denying architectural classicism. The aspirations of the architects of the modernist school have lost their former brilliance, and merely become tools for lauding capitalistic wealth. Perrault, having come face to face with a big national project, was expected to work with architectural formalism. And through the project itself, the conclusion he must have come to was to identify the death of architectural formalism and to let it be a new formalism. There is no arrogance here, but a sense of humble emotion, as if kneeling for the dead, and in employing such gentleness, he communicates the fact to us.

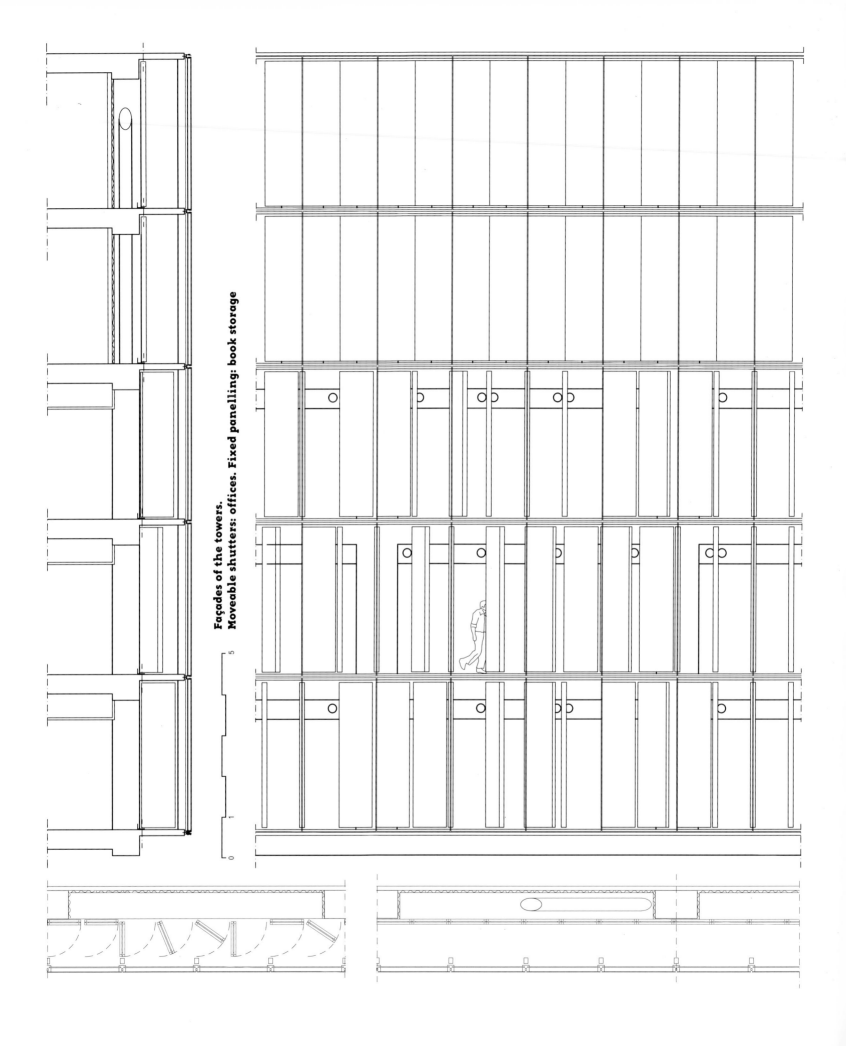

**Façades of the towers.
Moveable shutters: offices. Fixed panelling: book storage**

Marja-Riitta Norri

The forest in the library   "To embody character in a work is to use with efficacy all the means appropriate so as not to make us feel any other sensations than those that should result from the subject. To understand what I mean by the character or the effect caused by different subjects, let us consider the grand tableaux of nature and see how we are forced to express ourselves according to their action on our senses." Étienne-Louis Boullée, *Architecture* [1]

When, late in the 18th century, Jean-Jacques Rousseau criticized the results of technological progress, the destruction of nature and economic inequalities in society, his arguments were similar to those of today's critics of industrial societies. A slogan from two centuries ago, *back to nature*, seems understandable and justified in today's situation, for Rousseau's thinking does not imply a one-sided admiration of the primitive conditions: the aim is the unification of the interests of society and a natural way of life. In a corresponding way, the architects of the Enlightment attempted to reform the design of buildings. "Natural" architecture was based on classicism, which had been liberated from all unnecessary decoration into compositions of simplified, pure geometric form. The next step was the development of universal design methods and building typologies. "Nowhere else is there such a thoroughgoing and functional system of standards as in nature," was how Aalto expressed the principle of flexible standardisation in 1941. [2] The architecture of the Enlightenment was not, in fact, directly based on this, and neither has Aalto's organic thinking been put into practice since.

The huge dimensions of Étienne-Louis Boullée's projects may be compared to the Parisian *grands projets* of our own time. One of Boullée's visions is an enormous reading room, softened by ethereal light, for the Bibliothèque Nationale in Paris (1785). Kenneth Frampton has demonstrated its influence on the spatial planning of Henri Labrouste's library at Sainte Geneviève (1843-1850). [3] Labrouste's Bibliothèque Nationale (1857-1867) is experienced as an inside space whose identity is shaped by the elegant iron structure of the interior and the light that flows from above; the façades are more conventional, and do not stand out from the surrounding urban texture.

She has been Director of the Museum of Finnish Architecture since 1988. She established her own architectural practice in 1980, was editor-in-chief of *Arkkitehti - Finnish Architectural Review* from 1981 to 1987, and jury member of the 5th Mies van der Rohe Pavilion Award for European Architecture in 1997.

The architecture of Dominique Perrault's national library works in precisely the opposite way. Its effect is based on the building's position in the urban landscape, and the spatial experiences it achieves above all on the multidimensionality of the external spaces. The exterior is experienced as an advancing and changing process. In the approach to the building, one's view is dominated by the four book-towers that rise from the podium which, as a result of their carefully considered proportions, look distinctly smaller from close up than from a distance. The book stores, which take the form of open books, recall the prophecy of an archdeacon of Paris's Notre Dame, as interpreted by Victor Hugo, according to which architecture — that "strong and durable book of stone" — would lose its cultural position to the "still stronger and more durable printed book."[4] Perrault has, in a concrete way, achieved a successful symbiosis of these two competing cultural spheres.

As a climax to the ascent of a monumental wooden stairway, a surprising view opens up from the upper level of the heart of the library: a sunken pine forest in the central courtyard. This is no conventional urban park, but a piece of Rousseauesque wild nature, a symbolic "primal forest." The forest affects the atmosphere of the library's internal spaces and emphasizes the functional starting point of the reading rooms, silence, the microcosmos formed by the union of man and book. It affects the entirety of the inner courtyard, in which other natural phenomena also begin to take on greater importance: natural light changes the form of the built external space through the course of the day.

The forest can be examined from at least two opposing viewpoints. For northern peoples, it is a holy place through which the union between man and nature is concretely felt. The Helsinki architect Aarno Ruusuvuori, known for his minimalist, lucidly functionalist designs, spoke in the early 1990s of his need to escape from time to time to the forest, "to dig my feet into the earth and stand there like a pine tree, listening to what the earth could tell the soles of my feet. That kind of contact with the earth was an absolute necessity; without it, I could not have functioned at all."[5] From the point of view of utility, wood is the raw material of paper and thus also of traditional literature — even if printed characters are now being transformed into immaterial electronic impulses. Processed wood also makes its mark on the interior architecture of the library, outside on the upper level and steps, in the rotating panels of the book towers – where, however, it is reduced to veneer covering the surface of the metal structure.

The juxtaposition of the library's clear, reduced volumes, free of all decoration, with the forest demonstrates the truth of Sverre Fehn's notion that it is contrast that gives rise to a living dialogue between architecture and nature. [6]

I can never walk in the
primal forest, my steps are not permitted
to sink into the delirious green moss, my embrace
does not encompass the fallen, mouldering trunk,
but sometimes in such moments,
coal-black against the white, I
record the short delights
that I would like to share.

Pentti Saaritsa, *Bagatelles*, Opus 16, 1991

1 The quotation is from Anthony Vidler, *Claude Nicholas Ledoux, Architecture and Social Reform at the End of the Ancien Regime* (The MIT Press, 1990).

2 Göran Schildt, ed., *Alvar Aalto Luonnoksia (Alvar Aalto Sketches)* (Otava, 1972).

3 Kenneth Frampton, *Modern Architecture. A Critical History* (Thames and Hudson, 1992).

4 The quotation originates from a chapter entitled "Ceci tuera cela," which was added to the eighth volume of *Notre Dame de Paris*; here it is borrowed from Juhani Pallasmaa's article "The Two Languages of Architecture – Elements of a Bio-cultural Approach to Architecture," *Abacus* 2 (Museum of Finnish Architecture, 1992).

5 Aarno Ruusuvuori, "Structure is the Key to Beauty," *Five Masters of the North* (Museum of Finnish Architecture, 1992).

6 Sverre Fehn, "The Poetry of the Straight Line," *Five Masters of the North* (Museum of Finnish Architecture, 1992).

Furniture and steel fabrics for the Bibliothèque nationale de France **Paris, 1995**

In a library, arrangement is a fine art.

From classification to referencing, everything is named and numbered.

Numbers and letters indicate the reading room, the reader's seat, the authors' names or the material under study, the shelf, the bookcase and the bookstacks.

One could describe the library as a building, an architectural work of imposing size, its different buildings forming a "whole," or as something reconstituted from its key element, the furniture which, set out in a particular order, establishes the nature of the place.

Our understanding, perception, grasping of the library is organized around the furniture, however large or small it may be. A natural extension of the architecture, it plays a part in the *genius loci* in creating an inner life/townscape, with its streets, alleyways, squares, its nooks and crannies.

In these spaces for meeting or for privacy, made of wood panelling or solid wood, of fringed or seamed metallic fabric, cosseted beneath a gentle, indirect light or enlivened by bright spotlights, all wordly knowledge is peaceably consulted, exchanged and increased. **DP, 1995**

Stephan Kufferath

The development of metallic fabrics for architecture and design In 1992 GKD – a leading weaver of woven metals with manufacturing units in Germany, the USA, Spain and South Africa – established a first contact with Dominique Perrault, endeavoring to assist this famous as well as innovative architect in his interest and research on woven metals for use in architecture, particularly focussing on the interior design of the Bibliothèque nationale de France. On previous projects Perrault had already worked with synthetic fabrics, but for the Library only non-inflammable materials, such as metallic fabrics, could be accepted.
Interesting technical aspects of stainless steel meshes were discovered, such as resistance, durability, rigidity under tension, maintenance, acoustic qualities, etc. Metallic fabrics often solve several functional problems at once, problems that the architect would otherwise have to deal with one by one.
In addition to these purely functional aspects, design questions and aesthetics came more and more into play: the mesh's light reflection properties, the silk-like elegance of the material, the variable semi-transparency, and the GKD-specific ability to weave these fabrics in extra-large pieces, up to 8 meters wide. Dominique Perrault was led to comment: "These large fabrics interested us as a new architectural idiom, finally freeing us from the need to use large numbers of discrete modular elements. With these large pieces of fabric, we obtained surfaces that could be hung wall-to-wall, wall-to-ceiling, unified and seamless. This underscored the architecture, creating places that are, metaphorically speaking, hollowed out, continuous, unassembled. An architecture of sculptured masses." The discussions we had with Dominique Perrault from the very beginning of our joint work and research gave us a completely new vision of our product, and at the same time set us new technical challenges. Wire-weaving companies are used to dealing with very tight tolerances; precision with regard to mesh size, wire diameters, flatness of the fabric, are standard requirements of such industrial clients as automobile makers, aircraft companies, the food industry and the like. Perrault's approach was different: he wanted to stress the liveliness and irregularity of a woven fabric. Consequently, Perrault guided us towards product modifications corresponding to architectural requirements. During many months

He studied Business Administration at Cologne University, from which he received his Ph.D. in 1983.
Since 1984 he has been Managing Director of GKD, the manufacturer who has collaborated with Dominique Perrault in the development of steel fabrics.

of very close and intense interactive testing, Perrault and GKD experimented with many different mesh sizes, wire shapes, wire diameters, cables and threads in order to endow, as Perrault said, "the meshes with a form, a design in the manner of fashion designers."

The first test work that GKD carried out for Dominique Perrault was not in the Library, but in the Archives départementales de la Mayenne in Laval, France. Perrault designed a huge curved ceiling-to-wall application which is still cited today as a prime example of the optimum use of metallic fabrics in buildings. After that we concentrated on the ceilings of the Bibliothèque nationale de France, which resulted in various types of ceiling, undulating or taut, made from different mesh types, but always corresponding to the different rooms. Altogether, GKD has supplied for the Bibliothèque nationale de France about a dozen different mesh types for a dozen different applications in the building. Starting with this, GKD has answered the demands of various other architects and projects in all parts of the world. This proves that the basic research work initiated by Dominique Perrault was going in the right direction. The more we continue our research, the more we discover further technical, functional and aesthetic characteristics in the product. This confirms our opinion that metallic fabrics in architecture will be around for much longer than if they were a mere fashion trend.

Our work with Dominique Perrault has continued with his enormous Olympic projects in Berlin. The approach here has been completely different. To spread a giant table cloth over two tables in a garden, while at the same time giving them the light-reflecting quality of water in a lake, was difficult for us to imagine at first. These projects displayed Perrault's incredible creativity and imagination once again. We followed him technically, but only really understood when we saw the fantastic result.

At present GKD is working with Dominique Perrault on several new projects. Perrault never copies anything from the past; he seeks to go further, but in a different direction. We are happy to think that thus far we have only gone a few steps along the road which stretches before us.

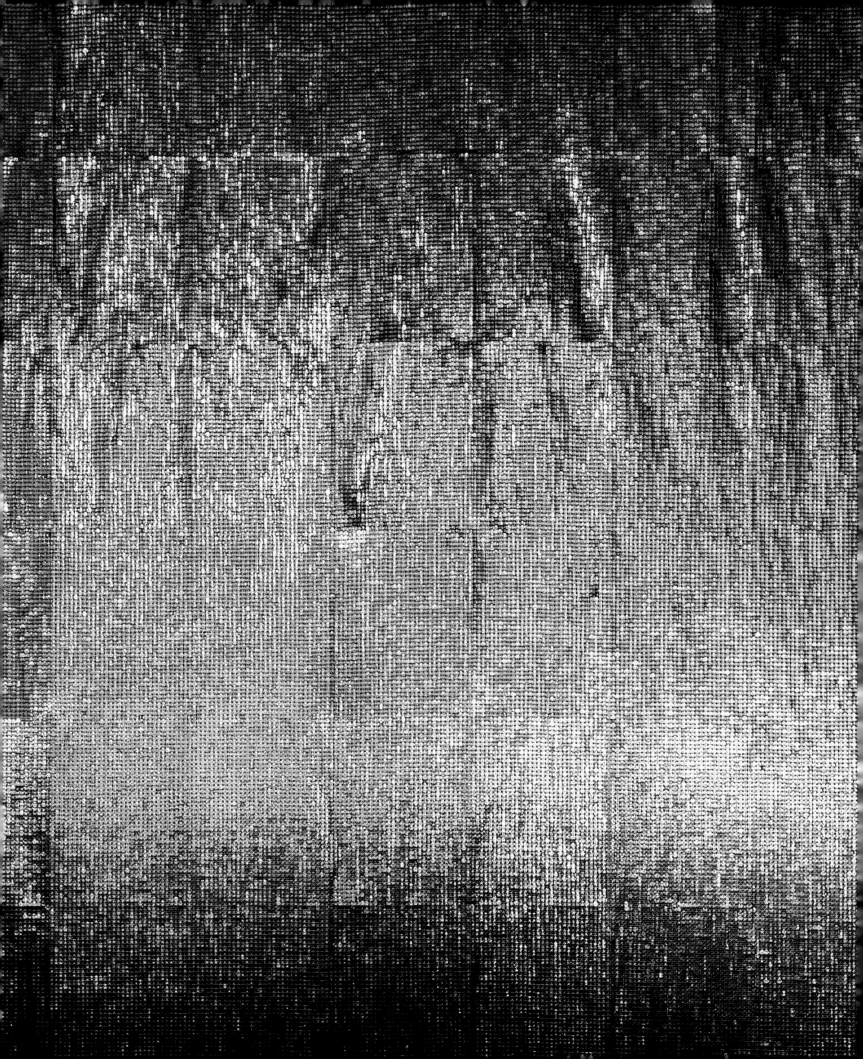

PROCESS TIMES

The brief remains the somewhat dry expression of the requirements of the developer. Because his intervention derives from a decision, the architect's input provides a response which goes beyond the question; it involves the formulation of a meaning that exceeds the basic prerequisites of the project's definition. The brief, a simple setting-out of the undertaking, and the constraints of the location constitute a set of requirements, of bits of information that are complex, yet which paradoxically create a time scale, a distribution of skills, of areas of intervention that must be subverted. In reality the completed project breaks free of the brief, displaces the simple normalization of functions and floor areas.

Thus, the Hôtel Industriel Jean-Baptiste Berlier, an innovatory business center, was beyond the customary competence of the developer, and in the end the idea of an open floorplan was finally accepted. Likewise, the Bibliothèque nationale de France was designed without a detailed brief, and the project was really developed jointly by doing away with the archaic notion of a fragmentation and hierarchization of knowledge. There is already an architectural "overdoing it" in the notion of a brief. For example, in the Vénissieux library project the librarians formulated their demands in a very precise way. A dialog was then initiated on the wider general organization of the project, which led to an ongoing evolution of the building's definition.

The work must be carried out simultaneously in all the dimensions of the process, and it is necessary to reinvent more adequate tools, a language and responses for each project. The contractor's traditional procedures must be revised, and this conceptual independence permits one to propose interventions which are progressively evaluated, optimized, along with the client.

A cultural exchange with the developer must be privileged in order to preserve varying degrees of freedom in the transformation of the design, so as to make extremely rapid changes in real time.

This is true at the moment of establishing dealings, at the moment of on-site work. This capacity for instant change without sacrificing the coherence of the design is conceivable because, at the base of work, each element of the conception remains autonomous.

Even if the solutions proposed turn out to be inadequate at first, this can lead to a more interesting solution than the one first thought of. For one of the façades of the Bibliothèque nationale de France, it was necessary to work for months on the design of glass ribs, and the more the work progressed the bigger the ribs were becoming. It was necessary to stiffen them, it was necessary to devise steel structural elements, because to produce 14 m-high pieces proved impossible. What finally emerged was a kind of orthopedic device whose glass was so thick that it lost all transparency and paradoxically created the effect of a wall. In the end this proved to be a negation of the initial hypothesis, which foresaw a kind of luminous skin. In just a few hours a solution using steel alone imposed itself. These opaque steel ribs, which however give the effect of a reflection, have created a much more precise effect of a curtain of light. The façade is now more intangible, lighter than if it had privileged the glass. This experience reinforces the idea that we must leave the availability of knowledge and technique unobstructed, that we must use them as an extension, a potential that is only realized within the unique context of the work process. Such an open-ended practice argues for architecture as an experimental field in which each building is a sum of experiences, out of which the project is formed, realized. In opposition to a "science" of architecture in which the procedures are fixed, arrested, here the propositions remain as hypotheses which are being permanently tested, verified or invalidated by the real nature of the work undertaken with one's collaborators. This is the real meaning of construction work. The first researches into the Bibliothèque nationale de France began with simulations, technical and financial studies, which allowed us to develop a sort of combined expertise. Given the very tight time frame, the question was to get the site moving, independently of the the ideas that were going to arise around the implementation. Faced with the hole for the foundations, the main contractor thought that the building was going to cover this enormous gap over and keep the outer walls in position. Nevertheless, the opposite decision had been taken, and after building an outer wall 14 m-high, one million cubic meters of earth were removed. In the space thus formed we set up a building which had no structural relation to its surroundings, in such a way that the constraints of the one do not handicap the other in future terms. These combined procedures develop in parallel to each other, and constructing a container for the building finally led the different companies involved to accept the realization of works that were independent of each other, but which in the end made up a whole. Such sequentialities offer a freedom, a flexibility in which constant modification is possible, in which one action is not prejudicial to another, but instead, due to their mutual independence, supplements it.

Fixed procedures lead to a certain dogmatism. Instead, the notion of process seems absolutely contemporary; it defines the idea of a collection, but also of an integration of procedures into a conceptual understanding of architecture. It's the separation between conception and realization that becomes blurred, that deviates from an idealist vision of the architectural project.

Transformations and developments consistently foster reflection and action. Even necessity is integrated as an effective factor of determinacy. Safety problems, say, which obviously condition a project, provide a material capable of giving breadth and fresh dynamism to questions about the design. It's a matter of permanently transfiguring these constraints into an alchemy. Such a notion of process also appears as something essentially didactic, since it encourages other people to participate. If we limit ourselves to a traditional, academic discussion in which each of the participants on the project enunciates his or her demands or needs and the architect rejects them, then dialog has not taken place. The architect who protects himself from these questions by refusing to countenance them demonstrates his weakness, his ineffectiveness, a certain incapacity. If the response is really participatory, the interlocutor pinpoints aspects of the procedure that he understands. In this way, common solutions emerge which augment the coherence and specificity of the project. We must encourage this work to be shared out and present the architecture as an evolving process. Architecture must be made through open dialog, it must be a table around which everyone may sit. There will not be any exclusions if the entire history of the project is mapped out and bundled with all the information to hand. This doesn't just mean, however, a participatory architecture according to the still humanist credos of the sixties. Instead, the complexity must be accepted of the processes of decision-making within the industrial world. Faced with our presuppositions, the question is to unlearn – we have to free ourselves, procedures must become legible and all the elements involved must be used for what we may think they are. There is no truth in architecture, in its language, its savoir-faire; the whole exercise is an attempt to leave such a notion behind. An early competition design for the Châteaudun factory (1981) still revealed an architecture made up of syntactic elements, a sort of collage with an extremely analytical background. This first confrontation with construction elicited the desire to depart from, to defy, a system of organization that produces objects with a clear identity, which are limiting.

This notion of process, of operation, is the only truth. It is what we call a project. DP, 1998

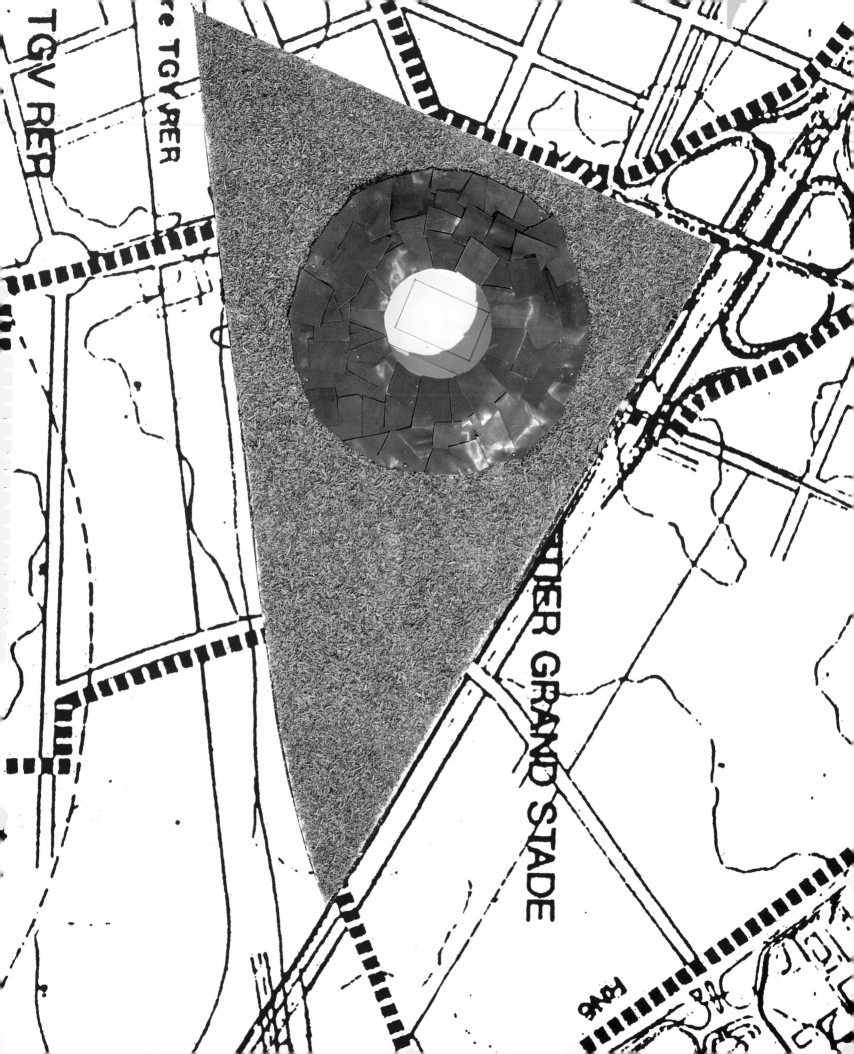

The Grand Stadium Melun-Sénart, 1993

The center of the new town of Melun-Sénart is criss-crossed by a dense complex of motorway and rail systems, with their interchanges and switches. Their impact is extremely constraining to the harmonious development of an urban fabric, but also highly necessary for a town he endowed with life.

Based on a reading of the town's forms and layouts, we can conclude that the stadium's context is of primary importance in defining the entrance to the town center, and acts as a sign or reference point as the town is crossed along the motorway. Nevertheless, its strong presence and the functions it houses ought not to disturb the life of the town, but work alongside it. The presence and absence of the stadium is the urban issue at stake – a "squaring of the circle" that must be resolved.

The presence of a major sporting facility on both a national and international scale, which will bring media attention to Melun-Sénart, and thus a bit of life and recognition for the town vis-à-vis the planning of the region. Absence of the same wished-for sporting facility when empty and when it neutralizes, with its immense retinue of parking lots, a vast central area of the town. A wish to conceal it.

The urban parti seeks to integrate, in one and the same stretch of landscape, four giant facilities: a motorway interchange, a vast stadium, the training stadium, and thousands of parking places. Proceeding from the idea of landscape handled in a contemporary way, without ecological complacency, but with a respect for all that is precious in the town center – namely, empty space – we have constructed a symbolical form which grounds the town around a natural site. The idea of landscape in the wider sense, of the rediscovery of Nature and Town, seems to us to be the locus and the link that will combine to create an identity proper to Melun-Sénart. **DP, 1993**

◀ **Preliminary study**

Lu Jia Zui Business District Shanghai, 1992

The study for the development of a major business district in Shanghai in the Lu Jia Zui district in Pudong is one of the great urbanistic reflections of our times. Our approach draws on the lessons of history, without excluding all the positive factors concerning the building of cities, whether they are ancient, modern or contemporary.

At the outset, it is necessary to perform a historic reading of the city's layout. This shows that Shanghai is defined by routes running from North to South and from East to West, forming a relatively orthogonal fabric. This factor determines the general orientation of the networks of the new district so that it can be naturally linked to the existing city, and furthemore, to a comparison with other cities which provide elements of reference in order to assess the scope and needs of the project.

The historical and functional analysis of the city cannot give account of the symbolical dimension of the "founding event" which must inscribe the new district within the landscape of the city. This "founding event" must mark the development of the historic city center, of crossing over to the other bank which holds a new identity for the "heart of Shanghai" by establishing another relationship between Town and Nature.

Opposite the river Bund, following its meander, we propose a broken line set at right angle, facing from north to south and from east to west. This solitary and unique form is in counterpoint to the architecture on the other bank, like the yin and yang. It provides a great park at the water's edge, and its rosary of high-rises acts as a support for the development of Shanghai towards the east. Just like a furrow in a field, this set square traces the plan of the new town. There will be room for two million square metres of offices, areas of activity or commerce and, beneath them, there will be a road network for cars, car parks and two additional tunnels joining both banks.

The whole project is designed in terms of duration, of time passing, of the slow creation of our cities' landscape. This research could be called "Towards a living urbanism," more interested in the void, in the in-between rather than on things themselves. We must protect the void, it is the city's most treasured possession. It enables the creation of places, it ensures the future of our cities, it guarantees the presence of nature. The void is immaterial, it is nothing, yet it constitutes "the foundation of our towns." All our relationships, our glances and our hopes, are established through the void. **DP, 1992**

153

Joseph Belmont

The city of Shanghai has consistently spread to the west of the Huang Pu River, to which it relates by means of a magnificent urban waterfront: the Bund. In 1990 the city administrators decided to go across the river with a number of tunnels and suspension bridges – since built – and to construct a new city doubling the current capacity of Shanghai, called Pu Dong. This extension was intended to include a business district of some 3,000,000 m² – similar to the district of La Défense in Paris – for which the Chinese requested an advisory commission from France.
I was appointed to this commission, and we subsequently arranged to organize an international consultation to explore the different possible ways of developing this quarter: our objective was to avoid a type of urbanism subject to the play of economic forces alone. With this end in view, we called on four high-level architect-urbanists: one English, capable of schemes both realistic and original; one Italian, from whom we expected more intuitive and unusual ideas; one Japanese, from whom we anticipated the vision of a city of flows very different from our own European cities; and one French, for his solid and rational approach. Thus it is that Richard Rogers, Massimiliano Fuksas, Toyo Ito and Dominique Perrault intervened. From their work, plus that of a fifth Chinese team, produced an outline of architectural recommendations which were to serve as a basis for an urban study of the quarter. Dominique Perrault's scheme fulfilled all our expectations, and was received with great interest by the Chinese authorities. He envisaged a huge "wall" of skyscrapers dialoguing with the Bund from the other side of the river and accommodating all the offices called for in the brief. Alongside this screen, in effect a sort of filter, a low-rise town was organized around a large park. On the other side of the wall, vast gardens bordered the river. This enormous development was to emphatically structure the future city and also constitute its "founding act" (without which a new city cannot be created). It would visually link the future city to the ancient one and could, in the long run, symbolize the collective ambitions of the city of Shanghai at the dawn of the 21st century.

Architect, he has been Architectural Director of the French Ministry of Culture, President of the Établissement Public de la Défense and Head of Public Works. He has participated in several urban design consultations, among them that of the Grande Arche de la Défense and that of the Lu Jia Zui business district in Shanghai.

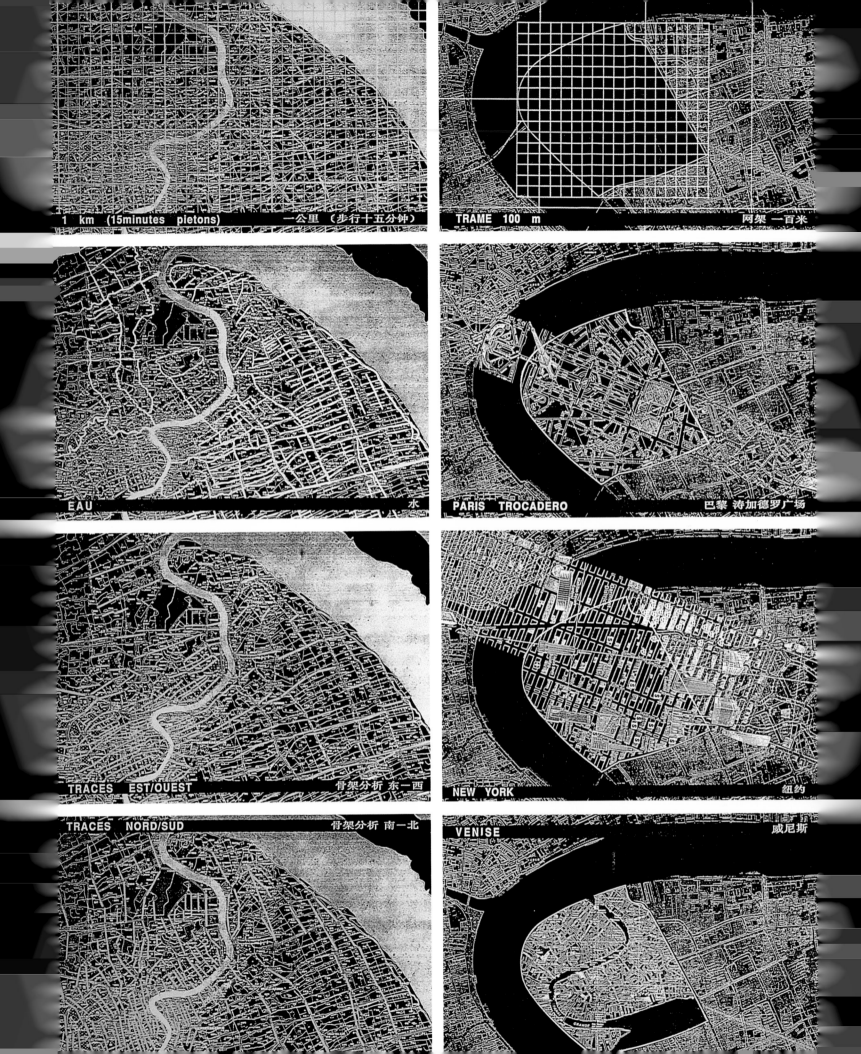

1 km (15minutes piétons) 一公里 （步行十五分钟）

TRAME 100 m 网架 一百米

EAU 水

PARIS TROCADERO 巴黎 涛加德罗广场

TRACES EST/OUEST 骨架分析 东一西

NEW YORK 纽约

TRACES NORD/SUD 骨架分析 南一北

VENISE 威尼斯

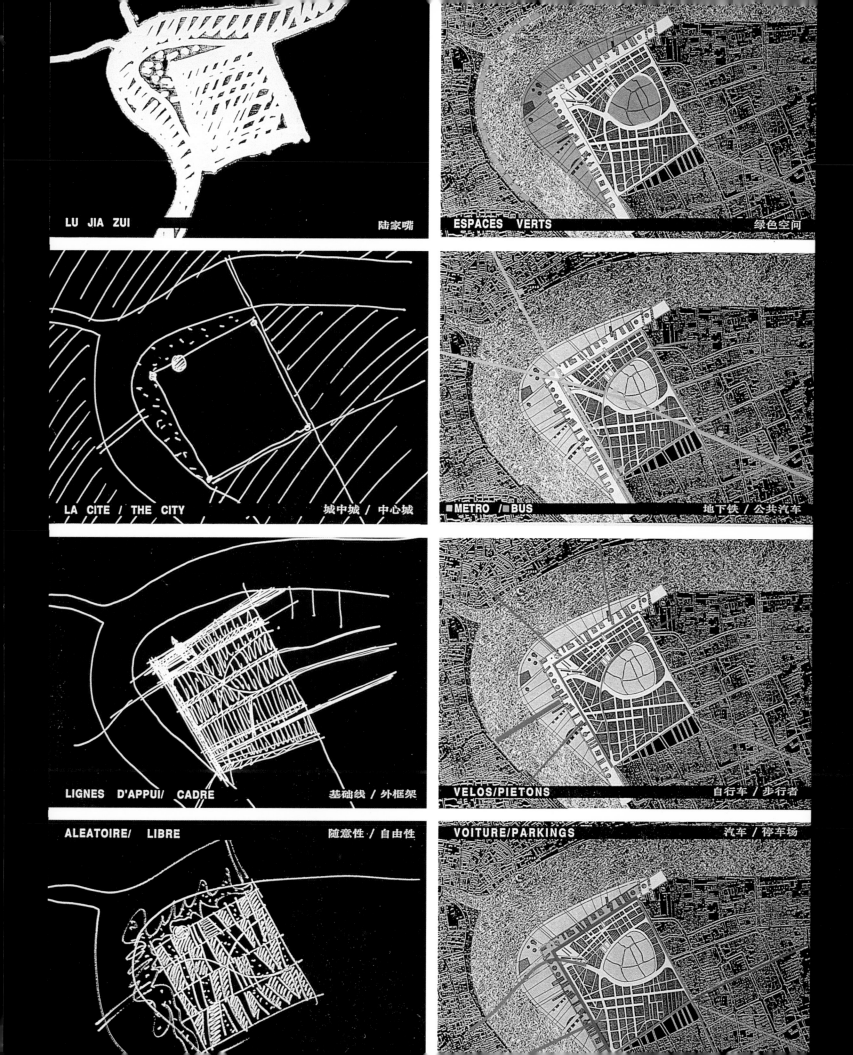

LU JIA ZUI 陆家嘴

ESPACES VERTS 绿色空间

LA CITE / THE CITY 城中城 / 中心城

■METRO / ■BUS 地下铁 / 公共汽车

LIGNES D'APPUI/ CADRE 基础线 / 外框架

VELOS/PIETONS 自行车 / 步行者

ALEATOIRE/ LIBRE 随意性 · 自由性

VOITURE/PARKINGS 汽车 / 停车场

Redevelopment of the Île Sainte-Anne

Nantes, 1992-1994

With the intention in mind of defining a method and an urban concept capable of orientating the future of the île Sainte-Anne, facing the historical center of the city and at the head of the Loire estuary, Mr. Jean Marc Ayrault, Deputy Mayor of Nantes, decided to set up a study group at the beginning of 1992.

The exploratory study aims, in the first instance, to bring together and organize the terms of reference which will orientate the debates and reflections such a subject raises.

This prospective approach bears, in fact, on an extremely important territory and on a set of risks that are particularly significant for the city and its river.

The proposals formulated are based on general analysis of the historical and geographical data, on the overall size of the site, and on diverse aspects of its landscape. They are also enriched by the examining of earlier studies and by the testimony of representatives of the institutions, different businesses and tenants' associations concerned.

The main objective here is to initiate a progressive and vital urbanistic undertaking, open to the contributions the future will bring, and exacting where the cultural and social values guiding future changes are concerned.

The thoughts that came up touch on the following issues:
- the location of the island
- the current nature of its urbanization
- the perspectives for developing its territory
- the question of urban definition
- methodological choices
- the organization of study and intervention.

Whatever the significance the île Sainte-Anne may have, it would surely be an error to implement a development project beside the existing districts. An overview is needed, one extending across the entire island. Few cities in the world have such a remarkable island. Equally rare are islands that are completely urbanized.

In Nantes this exceptional situation is currently linked to important development possibilities on the unused sites of former industrial and port installations. It is surely a commonplace to put forward the remarkable qualities of each project site. But the Nantes island hinges, more than any other risk-taking, on the trump card of a great project. **DP, 1992**

Study carried out in collaboration with François Grether

François Barré

Some bridges between architecture and art   Dominique Perrault is one of the few architects who attempts to draw new approaches to spatial perception from art and its procedures. Absolute ontological differences exist between art and architecture. Art is basically defined by gratuitousness, while architecture is oriented towards socialized production, towards social utility. This not to say that the procedures used by artists are at odds with architectural thinking and creation: the history of 20th century art reveals a generally developed questioning of space, a production in situ and a knowledge of architecture. On the other hand, architects know little, in general, about contemporary artistic creation.

The history of art as a whole poses questions about the relationships between reality, representation and the inscription in space. The investigations carried out by minimalism, Installation Art and Land Art into reality, into its effacement and its construction, recall the questions Dominique Perrault sets himself about the notion of presence, absence and disappearance. When he speaks of architecture, he often speaks of the moment an emotion appears. According to Francis Bacon, it is in the way in which the human being is absent from his representation that his presence truly appears, the trip-wires of reality, those moments in which movement and time topple over to reveal the body's wear and tear, caught in a dialectic of life and death. A moment which is both an absence and a presence, since one must imagine what is hidden. Dominique Perrault's work on the outside and the inside, the above and the below, is comparable to Jochen Gerz's, notably in the monument to the dead of Biron en Dordogne or in Sarrebourg and Harbourg. In his will to prefigure, Perrault seeks to demarcate and establish a narrative, but also a reference to the symbolic grand gestures of contemporary art, such as Joseph Beuys' planting of a thousand oak trees in Kassel. This way of playing on nature and architecture, on the vegetal and the mineral, links up with his research on presence-absence. The verticality of the Bibliothèque de France is only entirely readable in the visualization of a concealed central garden. In Berlin, on the other hand, the concealed verticality allows itself to be seen through a landscape in an orchard... One of the essential resources of the art of installation is to be found here: of considering that the trace sets up a counterforce which invents a narrative. In urban terms, one never ceases acting as a mediator between history and

Director of Architecture and Architectural Heritage at the French Ministry of Culture and Communication. Among his former positions, he has been President of the Institut Français d'Architecture, President of the Centre National d'Art et de Culture Georges Pompidou, President of the Grande Halle de la Villette and Deputy Director of the Parc de la Villette, and editor-in-chief of l'*Architecture d'Aujourd'hui*.

modernity, memory and project. In Land Art and Installation Art, working on space is an expression of the will to found a new reality on a pre-existing one, what Daniel Buren calls an "aesthetic of tension" and Richard Serra an "aesthetic of rupture."

A designer of cities and a Land Artist differ in their way of intervening on nature: the artists invent an archaeology, depict a future that might have existed, while Dominique Perrault modestly works on the traces: in them he finds a guiding principle which prevents him from falling under the absolute reign of design, of the predetermination of a city which would ask to be designed. When he speaks of working more with geography than with history, he poses a basic and problematic question: if the intervention on a city, that of the landscapist or the architect, consists in revealing the authentic nature of a space, that authentic nature is made up of history and geography. Academic historians and geographers like Yves Lacoste know well that geography is another way of making history... But what is to be done when the trace reveals a disorder, an evisceration, a dysfunction? Must one then complete the city by reproducing the preceding narrative in a way that also speaks of the taste and sensibility of the period? Or does one reveal the true nature of the place by inventing a fiction, in keeping with history and geography yet without reproducing a prior narrative — a fiction more credible than reality itself?

In Dominique Perrault there is also the maybe provocative love of saying that the architect's highest endeavor is to work towards architecture's disappearance.

This ambition goes beyond the form and categories of aesthetics, and refers to other value systems, those of emotion or those of construction and structure. Dominique Perrault is known for the extreme rapidity, at times the lightning nature, of his responses to architectural planning. In his urban interventions, on the other hand, he reiterates the need for time, for chance, which turns the city into both what one seeks to do and what is done. He experiments, swaps things around, assumes the risk of being modest, which is the accompaniment to, the acceptance of, uncertainty, without seeking to control it as an academic aspect of the building work... This is a highly promising approach, a guarantee of debate, of dispute... He is one of the rare architects to furnish elements of debate in an era that lacks spaces to confront the issues that concern us and the inventions that go with them.

Redevelopment of the UNIMETAL site
Caen, 1995-1997

The issue here is not so much historical, as geographical. The disappearance of an asset like the Société métallurgique de Normandie (SMN) can also create new opportunities which would help bring nature to the town.

To identify the assets and potentialities of the site and, proceeding from these, to define what the future might hold. Here, no vast layouts, no "new town," but the savage desire to connect and reconnect nature and architecture.

To detect three significant locations: the valley site, the plateau, the ridge. Along the River Orne, a wide avenue planted with beautiful trees asks for nothing more than being bordered by the continuum of buildings which defines a town. On the plateau, traces of the former SMN facilities guide and prefigure the lines interweaving contryside and urbanization. At the head of the valley, the layout of an old road which crossed the factory demands only to be linked to the neighboring areas of the town.

To attempt, then, to draw what is most essential from each location. To devise a wide-ranging project which will blend the different activities and, above all, be able to introduce other types of relationship with nature. The project attempts to qualify the locations by giving them an identity, a future.

The relationship between the plateau and the valley deserves protection, respect and enhancement. The problem is not an absence, but an excess, of ground. The redefinition of the town extends to the riverbanks and the hillsides and, from there, to the entire site. **DP, 1996**

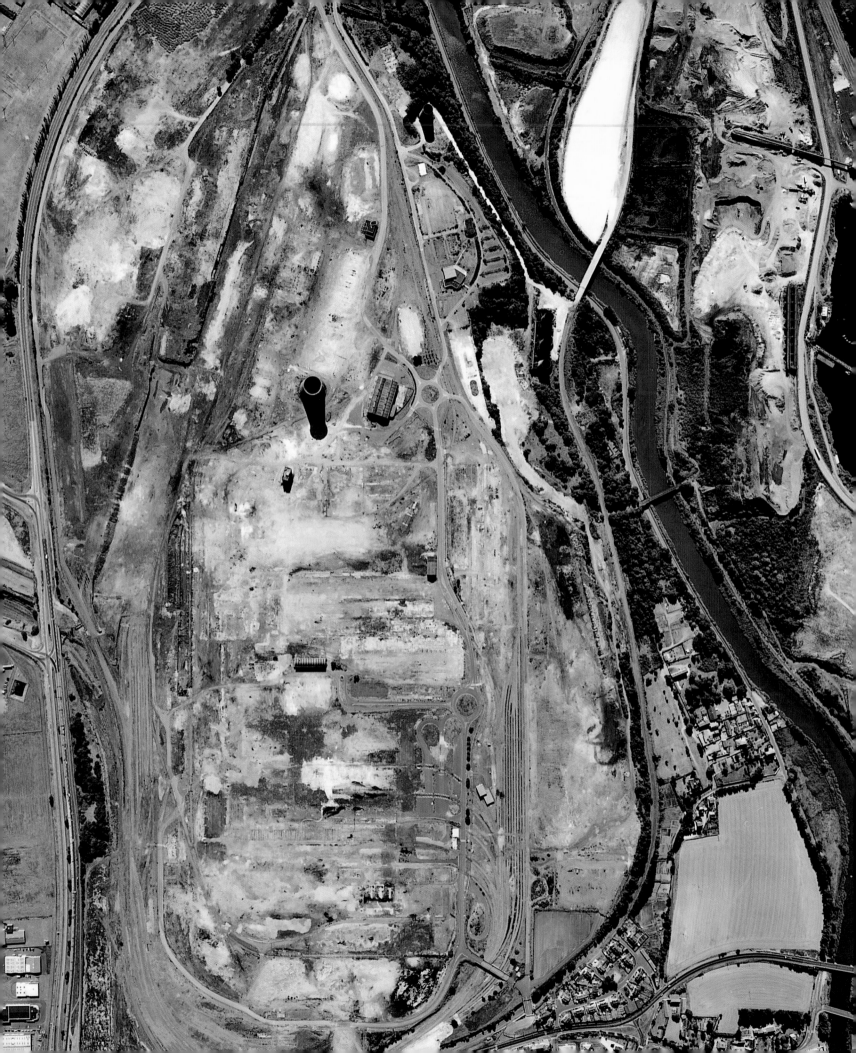

FORMS OF UNITY

All idea of a representation of forms aside, the box is a powerful element within architectural vocabulary, it seems to offer the possibility of a reassuring unity. Boxes are shelters, they have an immediately practical value which calls to something mythic, the protection of habitation, the myth of the originary house. This definition of a particular place leads directly to the question of a prohibition. Architecture does not affirm itself as an art of liberation. On the contrary, architecture creates separation. To construct is, by definition, to separate. An architect does not construct a unity, he organizes separations; physically, he separates. The box creates an enclosure; it will therefore accentuate this notion of a shelter without being, for all that, an enclosed place. The box, for me, is an ambiguous geometrical object which constantly suggests relationships between inside and outside; it is a generic object which, while being the instrument of separation, makes spatiality feasible. This paradox is something permanently exploited by an architecture which, in unilaterally defining the act of building as an act of separation, tends to invest it with a form of authoritarianism.

Our field of research must displace this generic function of separation in order to construct buildings that are more permeable, open to a greater degree of freedom and productive of ways of life which are not constrained.

In many of my projects, despite the repeated presence of such boxes, there is no formal unity to the envelope. Unity must be interpreted according to a notion of

Centre Technique du Livre

The site of the Centre Technique du Livre de l'Enseignement Supérieur is located immediately alongside the A4 motorway and the A line of the regional express rail link, which connects the new town of Marne-la-Vallée to the center of Paris in less than half an hour. The Centre is a conservation tool shared by the university libraries of the Paris region for part of their collections of scientific interest.

The buildings realized during the first phase are organized along the western edge of the site, so as to enable any future extension to spread in three directions: north, south and east. The compositional axis of the overall plan is a covered indoor street. Workshops and stores are organized along this line of force. Perpendicularly arranged to the north of the covered indoor street, a series of parallel buildings houses the workshops, offices, conference rooms and classrooms. The storage modules are located on the other side of the indoor street.

The façades, 9 meters high for the workshops and 15 meters for the storage blocks, are faced with aluminum panels, some plain and others with moveable slats.

A kinetic effect is produced by the alternation of these panels.

The indoor street has a glass roof, a source of overhead lighting.   **DP, 1995**

181

N↓

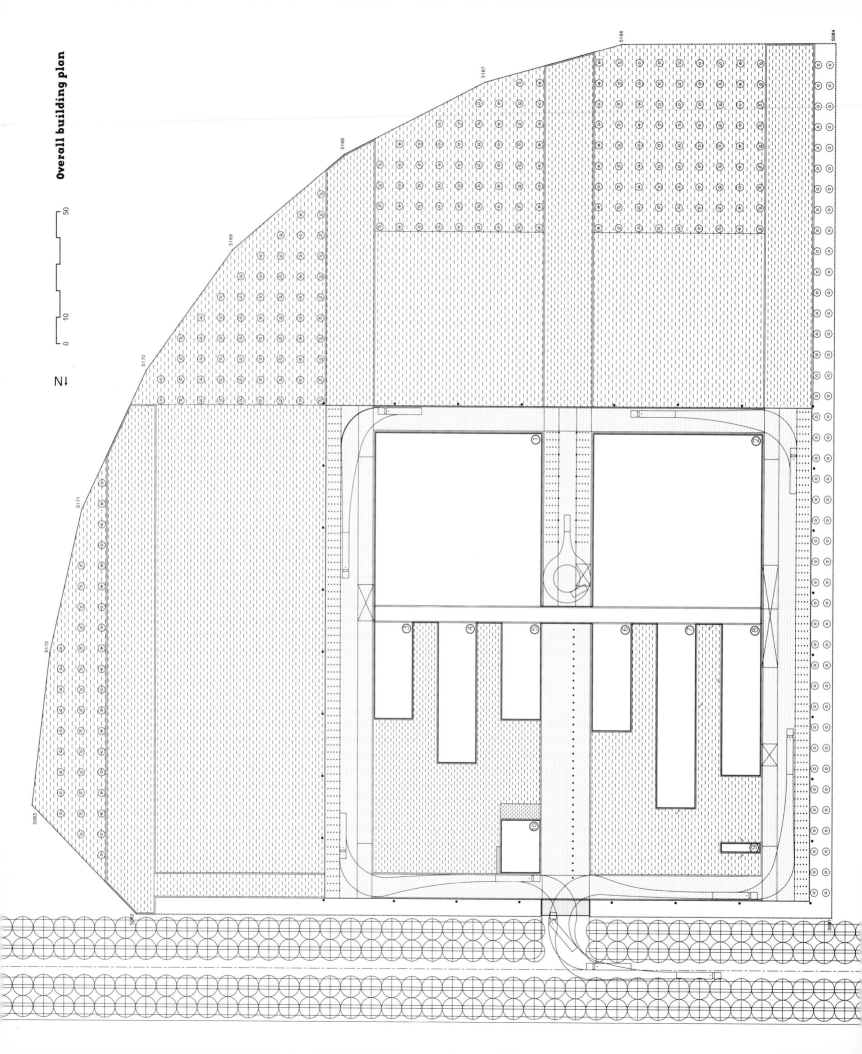

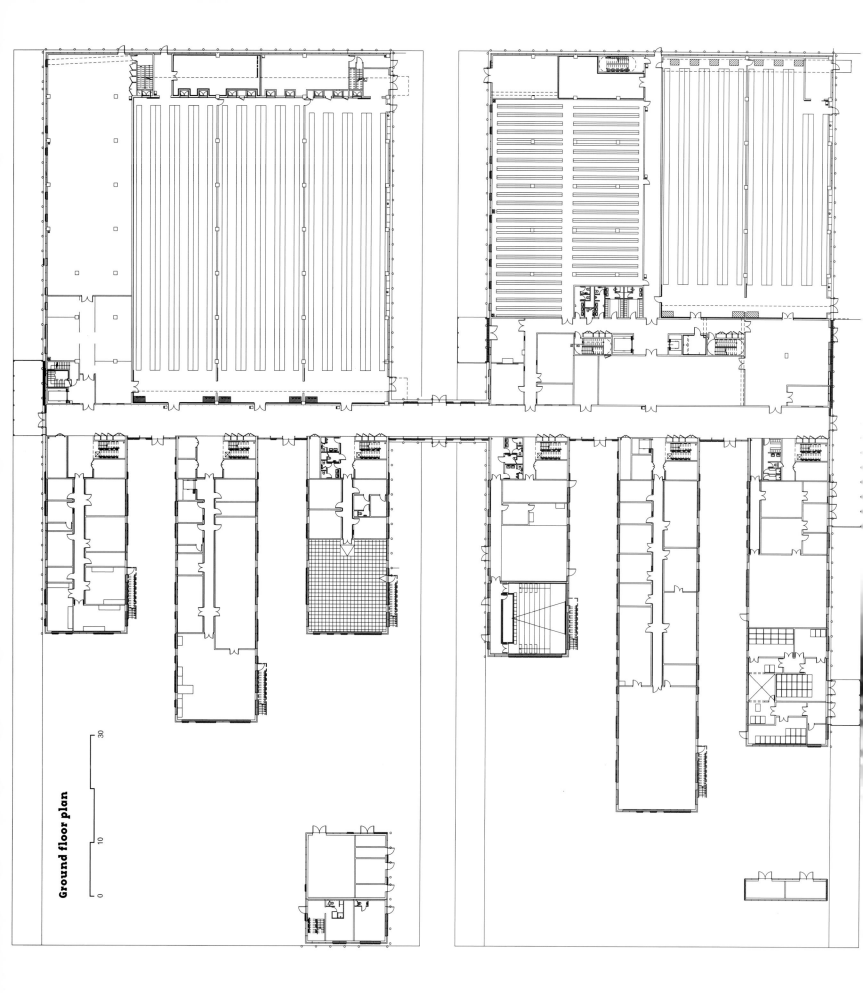

Ground floor plan

30

10

0

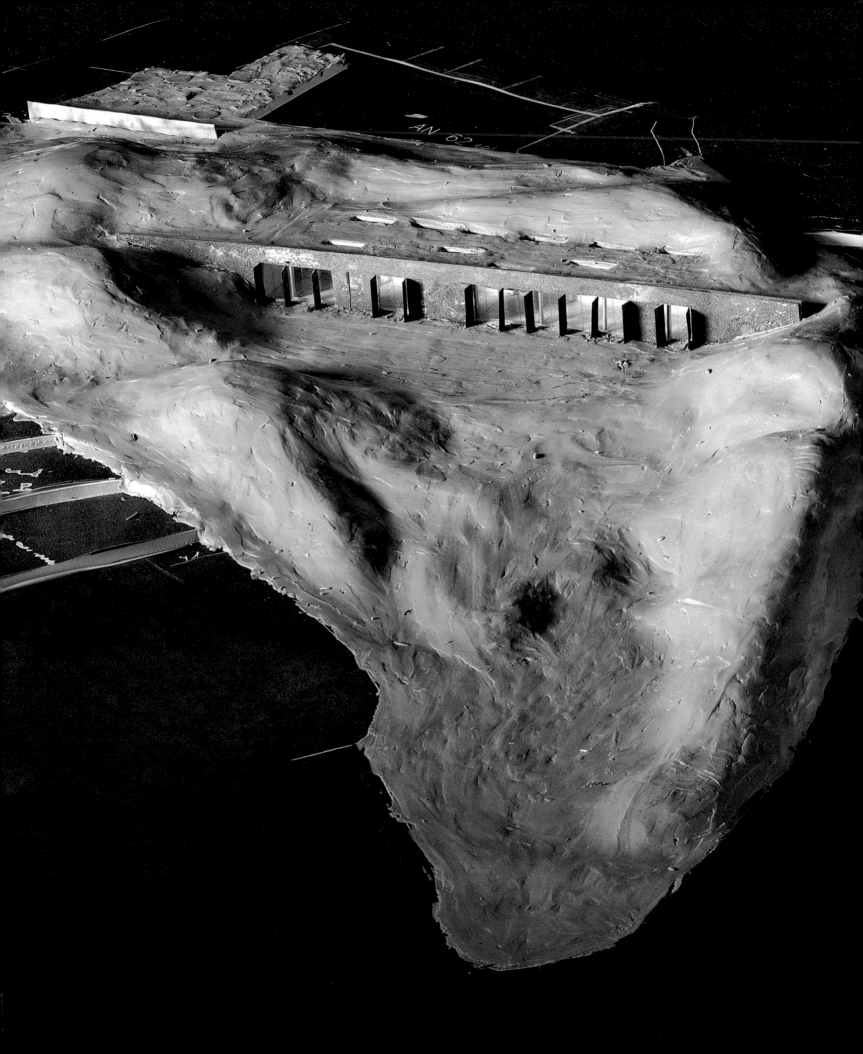

Villa Saint-Cast Côtes d'Armor, 1992-1995

This house, is it really a house? That's the question or self-questioning we've deliberately set ourselves.

Architecture's presence or absence is a persistent theme of reflection in our work, which is increasingly concerned with the question of LANDSCAPE as a linking element between ARCHITECTURE and NATURE.

Can one live underground? Can one rediscover the cave of humanity's earliest times as the subjective foundation of man's presence on the earth? This architecture is an experiment, a ceaselessly renewed experiment aimed at understanding, feeling, trying to live better with/in our surroundings. Such research into sentient emotions, which can be understood only by physically living them, makes one think of the idea the painter Francis Bacon develops with regard to emotion in painting, which ought to reach Man's brain without passing through his intellect. Genius loci, the INDIVIDUAL'S happiness: two good reasons for us, as architects, to build things, thereby showing that conventional commonplaces and preconceptions are not the only rules of ART
– to which the conformism of our contemporary societies too often refers itself. **DP, 1998**

Erik Orsenna

There are houses lacking an idea: the various rooms have been randomly put together and the life within their walls unfolds haphazardly.

There are also ideas lacking a house: stuck out in the cold and the coldness of impersonal concepts, you shiver inside them.

Even on the hottest day.

The architect has known how to combine ideas and heat. Better still, the loftiest radical thought and the freedom of each individual. With a malicious pleasure in playing with contradictions. Hence his house, as secret as can be, truly invisible, foisting itself on nobody, is also the most open I know: excavated in the hill, the house blends into it. Yet you could also say that the lawn stretching before it enters it like a gentle green tide. Likewise the extreme length of the immense "salon": you could feel lost there, even though at any one moment a set of moveable partitions enables you to create the space you want. As a voyeur fascinated by daily life, I can imagine, seen from outside, the events that imperturbably follow each other: a lady is ironing, some children are playing together, pets are snoozing, a fire crackles before a woman who is reading, a man draws at the far end of the room. Like the compartments of a train, modifiable at any moment, a train that rolls along in silence, akin to life itself.

Any house, waywardly or willfully, is a moral issue; that is to say, an intentional affair. And any half-measure is already a betrayal; that is to say, a laceration.

Comfort like this, born of audacity in north Brittany, has to be applauded.

Scholar and writer, he is a member of the Académie Française and of the Conseil d'État. He is also President of the Ecole nationale supérieure du Paysage, President of the Centre International de la Mer and Collection Director at the Librairie A. Fayard. From 1983 to 1985 he was Cultural Advisor to the President of France.

N↗

0 1   5

0   1   2

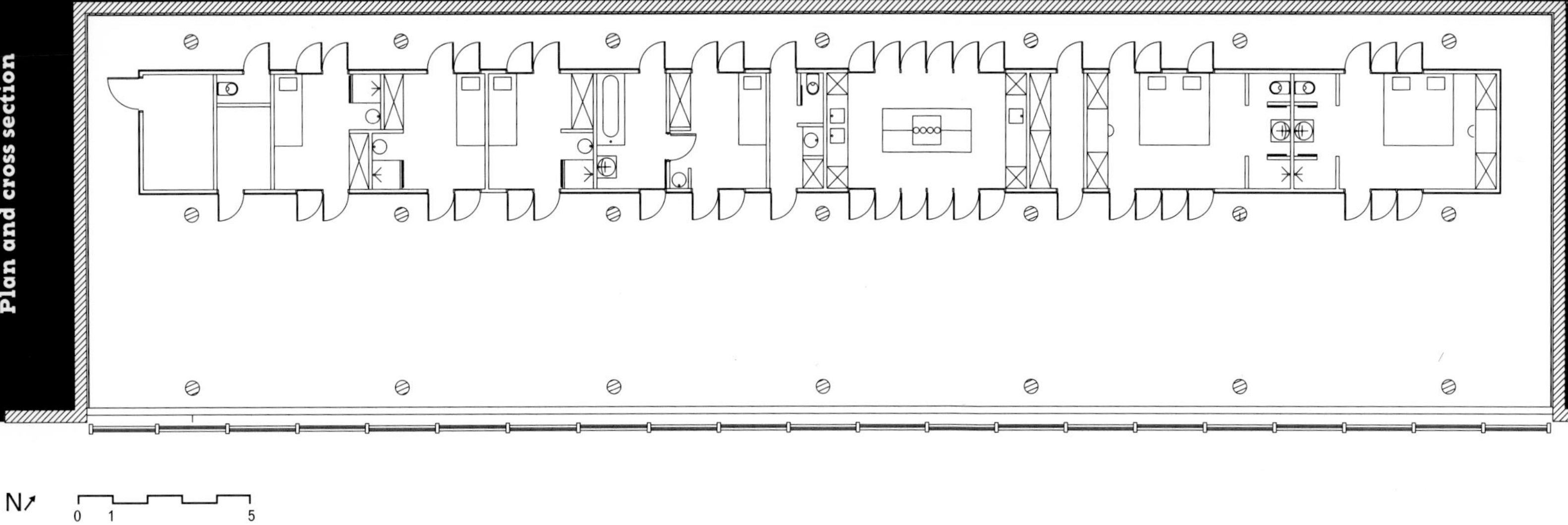

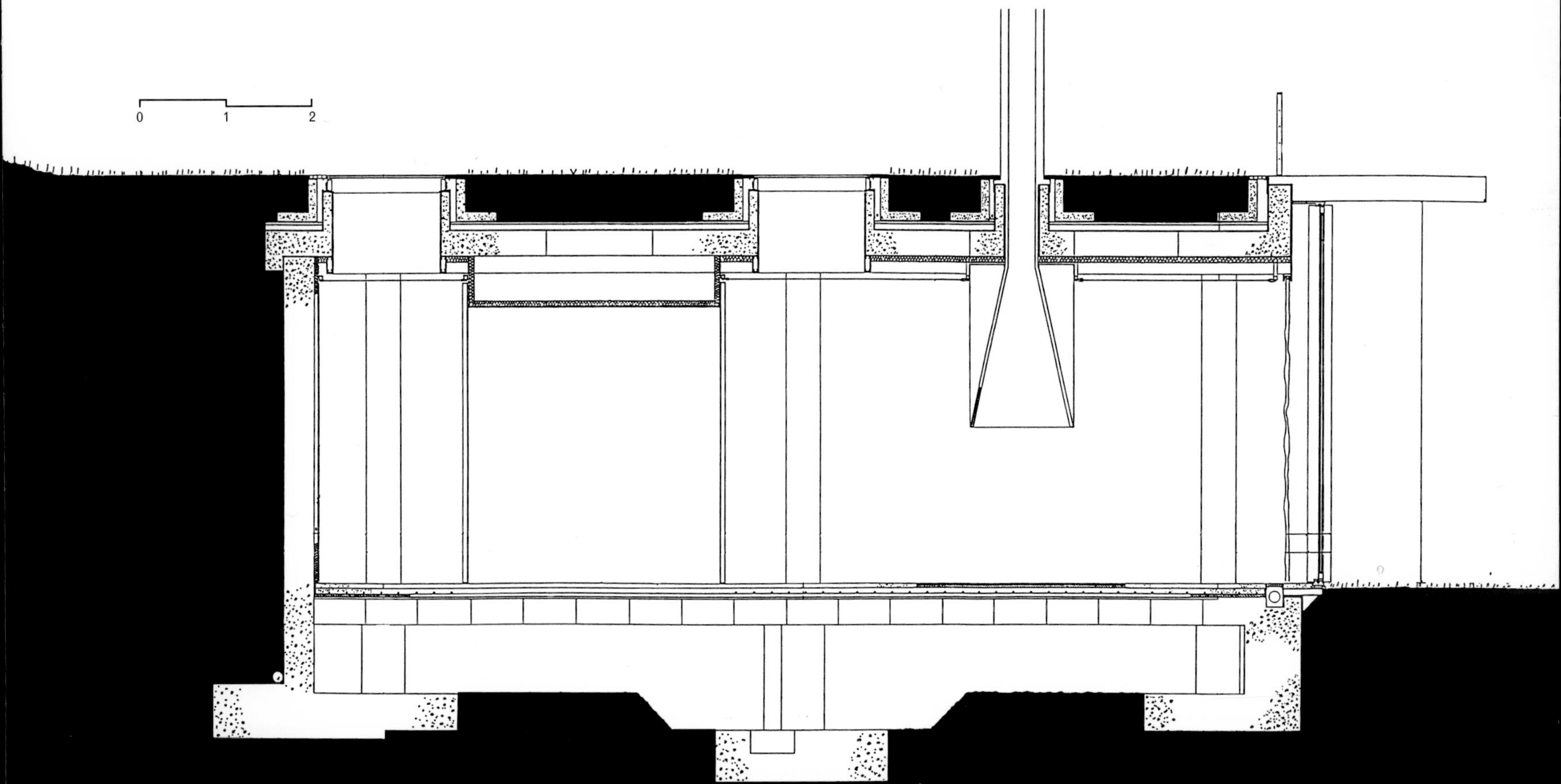

The Great Greenhouse

Cité des Sciences et de l'Industrie, Paris, 1995-1997

The general scenery consists in creating a protected space, "alongside the world," wherein a certain mystery reigns. Getting from the Great Greenhouse surroundings to the greenhouse itself comes about through a lower antechamber encircled by the hang of a curtain-like draping of fabric.

The symbolic elements of information and consultation are brought together and organized between the greenhouse flooring and that of the Cité des Sciences et de l'Industrie.

The detachment of the greenhouse thus offers two spaces, one for communication, the other for experimentation.

In functional terms, this scheme encourages adaptation over a period of time. Such freedom of development favors the updating of the collection and the regulation of public access.

The general scenery is ultimately linked to the functional consequences of this "magical" place, seeing that the Great Greenhouse is an instrument which has to be able to regulate itself in space and time.

For this reason the scenery takes the following main parameters into account:

– Access to the space is NATURAL.

Continuity and fluidity of the visitor's movement, thanks to the detachment of the Great Greenhouse from the ground level.

– The place is MAGICAL.

Autonomy of the experimental space as a living laboratory.

– The exhibition's identity is FACTUAL.

The fabric enveloping the greenhouse volume characterizes the exhibition space.

This presence is amplified by the diffused light emanating from the greenhouse itself.

– The technique is SIMPLE.

The technical facilities are mainly installed in the ceiling of the greenhouse and allow for all the required interventions of adaptation and maintenance. The greenhouse flooring is a receptacle for draining the water and forms a double watertight tank. The dissociation of the network constitutes the technical architecture of the system.   **DP, 1995**

Page 210: competition model Page 211: model of the commissioned project

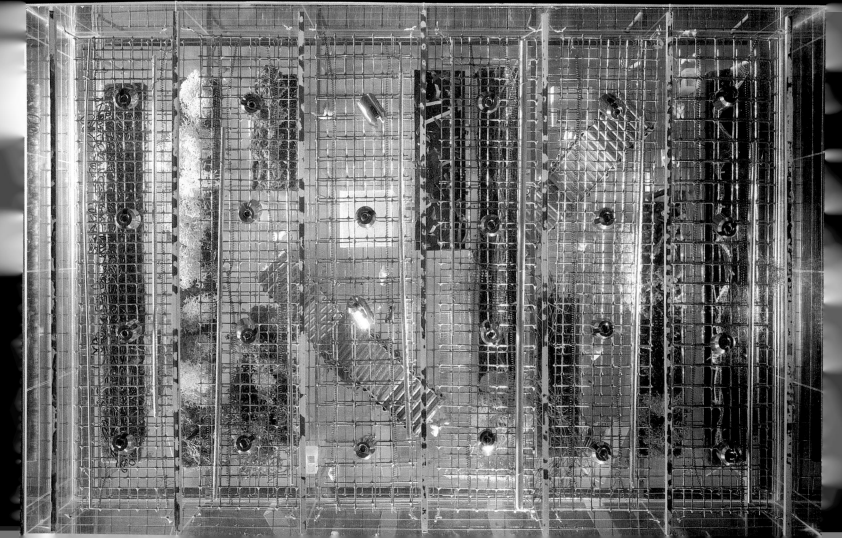

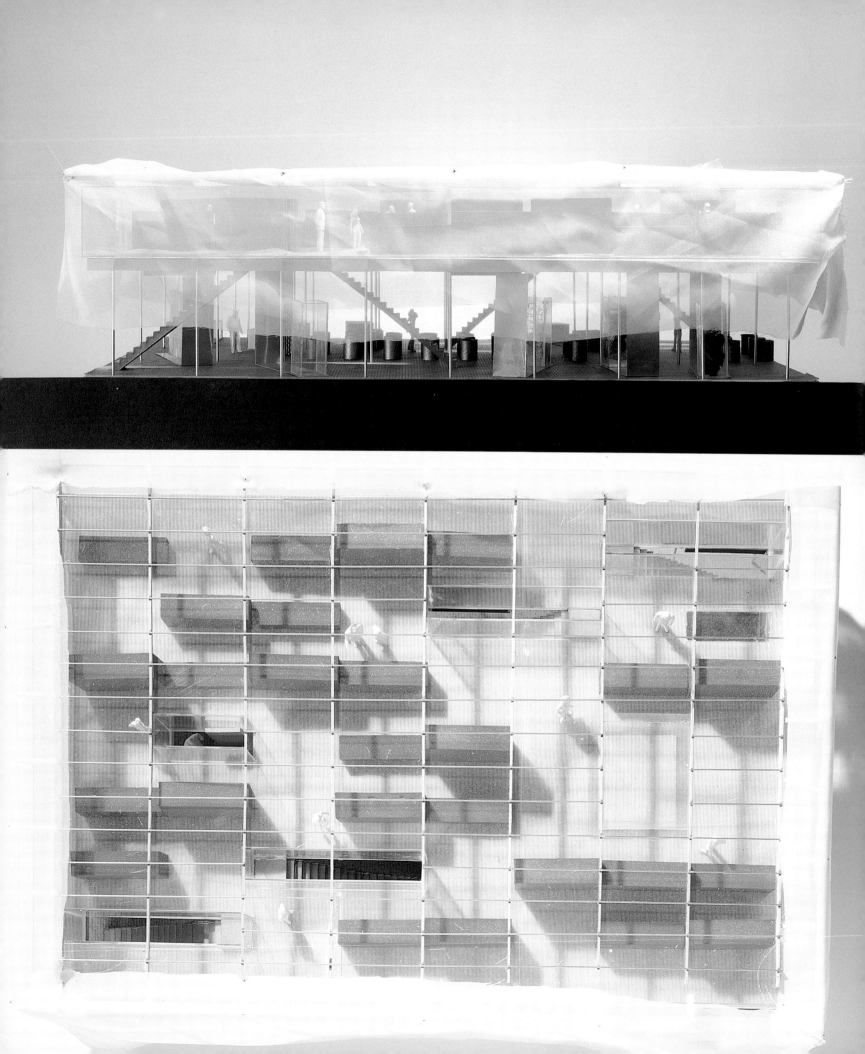

Alain Passard

Antonin Carême, chef of kings and king of chefs, used to say, "The Fine Arts are five in number, namely: Painting, Sculpture, Poetry, Music and Architecture, whose main branch is Pastry-making." The comfort and well-being of a chef lies in the construction of a working kitchen in which the work-table is transformed into a work-bench; at that point, knives and scissors become authentic tools.

The kitchen is the open fire, the rôtisseur's main ally: to cook is to sculpt the product with flame, a true conjugation of the cook's emotion and the fire's force.

The architecture of a dish is in the difference and superposition of textures and tissues: in cooking, knowing how to give a sauce an architecture is an art.

Like the architect, the cook chooses his materials and his volumes. To construct a dish is, by and large, to give it solid foundations through the quality and origin of the products. A great dish is also a line, a design with forms, height, transparency and light. And so, my dear Dominique, seeing you on the building site, we also imagine you in a kitchen and, in the shadow of the great architect that you are, a very good cook is to be made out.

Chef of the Restaurant l'Arpège, Paris, three stars on the *Michelin Guide* since March 1996, and Relais Gourmand on the 1999 *Relais et Châteaux Guide*.

Installation project for Francis Giacobetti's work HYMN

Paris, 1995

The project is an "installation" in the contemporary art sense of the term; that is, an intervention based on the placement of an object in relation to its environment. Without "touching" the environment, the presence of this "sensitive plate" organizes a place by endowing it with its particular symbolic "meaning."

Francis Giacobetti's HYMN is rendered in perspective, multiplied to infinity, so true is it that the intellect is varied, multiform and incommensurable; the intellect as "a bit of sky fallen to earth," hurled down from on high, embedded in the ground but still luminous, lightweight and immaterial. This plate vibrant with a thousand eyes (gazes), a thousand reflections, possessed of a thousand faces and rummaged through by a thousand hands, is the scheme for a magic and mythic place beside the Seine and at the foot of a monument subsuming all of Man's knowledge.

The plate consists of glass panels containing a layer of liquid crystals (the image) activated by a low-voltage electrical current. The plate is placed on slim steel columns which modulate the exhibition space.

The upper level of the plate is flush with the embankment. Four moveable metal footbridges are placed above the glass and cross over the plate and ponds. The itinerary at this level can be modified by moving the footbridges along the axis of the plate.

Metal stairways lead to the entrance to the exhibition space, which is four meters below the level of the embankment.

Inside, the walls and floor are of rough concrete (in contrast to the plate, a lightweight precision object).

The walls have built-in projection screens for films and images.

The floor directly below the plate is divided up into concrete slabs sensitive to the movements of the visitor. Each slab is linked electronically to a cell in the plate. The visitor activates a cell through his or her own weight, thus triggering a three-part series of images. Seen from above, the plate becomes an object full of moving images, the three-part series being activated and deactivated, according to the rhythm of the movements below. **DP, 1995**

219

Massimiliano Fuksas

Perrault: a radical architecture   Dominique Perrault's design for the
Geneva Center of Security Politics (GCSP) in the Place des Nations responds
perfectly – next to my "geography and landscape" project – to its setting.
On the east side, the Maison Universelle, and orthogonally from south
to north, Perrault's building. Immersed in the water, the transparent
outer skin causing it to almost hang in the air. Rigorous and meticulous,
"simple" architecture.

The clear, precise proportions construct the object.

We might even argue that this is an installation in a public space,
or a work similar to what sculpture, and not very often architecture,
expresses.

The rapport Perrault maintains with composition is far from being
academic: it is not a question, here, of balancing masses and weights,
but of taking a firm position and...sticking to it.

The choice, as I have said, is a radical one: it is the subsoil from which
the metal mesh and its thousands of vibrations springs.

Dominique Perrault is one of the few architects who knows how to choose
the "easy" part on which to articulate his composition. He does not make
any concessions to a simple aesthetic. He does not accept compromise.

His success lies, precisely, in not wavering before a mass of possibilities.

A concept is almost always at the base, a simple but never simplistic
vision around which to build a coherent series of "actions."

Close to contemporary art in this, Perrault is sensitive to all forms of
influence, and always puts his status as architect at the center of things.

To be sure, the world of the "installation" is perceivable in his work.

He feels a strong and admitted attraction for contemporary art, yet what

Architect and urbanist, he is the Director of the architectural section of the Venice Biennale. He has been a consultant of the
urban planning commissions of Berlin (1994-1997) and Salzburg (1994-1997), has taught at the architecture schools of Rome,
Stuttgart, Columbia University and Hannover, as well as in the Ecole spéciale d'Architecture in Paris and the Akademie für
Bildende Künste in Vienna.

this ultimately means is fostering his sense of precision and an obsessive attention to the "project."

Dominique Perrault's Geneva design is nothing like the industrial warehouse on the Paris *Périphérique*. The transparent architecture that retained the light and the fleeting images of the roadway there gives way, in Geneva, to the vibrations between interior and exterior and to the analogy between the two spaces.

This is, finally, not so much an object or "bachelor" architecture as *une pièce* in an urban landscape/geography.

If the glass box on the *Périphérique* has a strong connotation of urbanity, in Geneva it acquires an intensity which transforms any potential effect into one that is more radical and necessary.

Perrault investigates the territory of matter and not that of materials: he evaluates and establishes the degree of light absorption, or even of transparency, or in other cases texture...

All this contributes to turning an idea into a rigorous process.

The resulting image has a particular clarity which is inflected into simple details – lacking emphasis, naturally – in order to arrive, at last, at the heart of things.

Some designs, and this one in particular, make me think of the writing of "Albert."[1]

The construction is born of the relationship to ground and sky.

The rest, what we normally call a "building," has little importance. What matters is the silhouette, the skyline, and the *piano/pianissimo* way the ground is touched.

1 Édouard Albert (Paris, 1910-1968), who devoted much of his work to the lightness of structures.

THE SPACE OF EMOTION

In many projects the work carried out on the envelope of the buildings conditions and reinforces the interface in which architecture is at stake. The skin of a building, which usually relates to highly technological questions, seems to me to be more a matter of clothing, and it assumes a cultural value from that fact. The façade is no longer a limit, it is a transitory locus, a dynamic domain, and if transparency is involved, this is to accentuate the idea of a visibility that is not simply of the order of the gaze. Even if it involves seeing the life that is unfolding inside, this does not correspond to the idea of literal transparency.

If the facade does reveal, it is because it is an ongoing transcription of the life of the building and of the changes in its use. On the contrary, the advertising which increasingly covers the means of transport, the city's big buildings, is in part fascinating, spectacular, festive, and at the same time it ruptures the constituent relationships between interior and exterior. It returns architecture to the order of the image, it unilateralizes its legibility. It is necessary to leave this reductive field of vision behind in order to regain a truly phenomenal viewpoint. In purely geometrical terms, drawn in two dimensions, architecture appears solely as the product of a composition. The instant we move on to three dimensions – to empty space, matter, light – the only way of understanding it is emotional; this is not an understanding that can be intellectualized a priori. We go back, here, to that dazzling observation of Francis Bacon's, for whom emotion must reach the brain without passing through the intellect. Architecture must invest this space of emotion.

Materials, then, don't have a uniquely syntactical, objective and formal value.

A material is essentially effective in the relationship between matter and light; it does not enjoy the privilege of its physical

Redevelopment of the SULZER site

Over the centuries the town of Winterthur has witnessed easily identifiable urban changes that are inscribed in the landscape as a mixture of Town and Nature. One of the most determinant of these changes is the establishment of the SULZER Company on the edge of the Old Town. Today, the evolution of industry, together with the conditions of life in the center of Winterthur, are decisive factors for rethinking the urban structure. The existing problems do not seem to us, in fact, to be solvable by architecture or by the restructuring of buildings, but only by the setting up of large-scale public spaces. The project consists in creating a new town center for Winterthur based on the creation of a public plaza linking the SULZER site to the old town and introducing squares or gardens into the neighborhood.

Two founding acts can thus be defined: on the one hand, the PLAZA, and on the other, the renovation and raising in height of the SULZER Tower, a landmark of the town.

Four phases of intervention are proposed:

– the first phase, to work with part of the company's buildings,

– the second, to create multi-purpose buildings: dwellings, offices, workshops,

– the third, to organize the public spaces so as to end with the fourth stage,

– the redeployment of the station giving on to the central square.

These phases are, however, subdivided into sections promoting the thinking through and adaptation of the planning, renovation and building activities which will be retained. We are trying to create conditions favorable to the development of an urbanism that is alive and open towards the adaptations necessary to the evolution of our contemporary world.

The building designs presented here are not architectural designs but architectural concepts. **DP, 1992**

233

Wilhelmgalerie

Potsdam, 1993

REDISCOVERING THE CITY   The pleasure of "living in the city" has to do with walking around and meeting people. In order for that to happen, places are needed in the city which favor exchanges between people; in short, human relations.

The presence of architecture and of nature forms a poetic whole in the combination of a covered system of galleries or arcades with a central park opening onto the waters of the canal.

This organization of urban space forms a core for the neighborhood, gives the place an identity. In terms of urban design, the challenge is how to continue with the urbanistic principles that have founded the city (symmetry, axiality) while adapting them to the aspirations of our time and our way of life. From this point of view, the proposed site becomes part of a vaster organization which accounts for the history of the town and the creation of its public spaces.

The harmony of this Architecture rests on a classical "order" which marks the period throughout Europe. This stylistic quality has provided the town with some marvellous buildings.

This project is heavily inspired by the urban composition of the town's historic districts and the layout of its monumental façades.

Nevertheless, in order to respond coherently to the urban challenge posed by the competition, one needs to consider the layout of the Wilhelmplatz as a whole. The designer's assuming of this position may appear exaggerated at first sight, but one must bear in mind that the development of the European city has to be "conceived at the city scale" and not only within the specific property lines, as is the case in the renovation of existing buildings.

We are creating a park in the town center with views of the dome. This natural space is bordered by two galleries which house the program called for by the competition brief. Pursuing a contemporary reading of "the classical architectural order," we find the various retail outlets at the base of the building, beneath the colonnade, between street and garden. The offices are at roof level, akin to a crest forming the attic story. This layout evacuates the body of the building, and allows for views towards the garden through the colonnade. The existing trees will be transplanted on site to form the park's first plantations.

Time-wise, the project is easily realizable. It could be broken up into different phases, corresponding to the economic and urban situation of the town.   **DP, 1993**

Sebastian Redecke

Potsdam is situated to the south-west of Berlin and its structure is characterized by a harmonious Baroque expansion from the 17th century. The growth of the city continued under the Kings of Prussia, and among its most notable monuments is the famous Sanssouci Palace, summer residence of Frederick II. By the end of the Second World War, bombing had destroyed important areas of the city.

Precisely here, on this former Prussian stronghold, and ignoring its architectural past, the rebuilding program carried out by the German Democratic Republic was founded on the construction of enormous apartment blocks which completely ignored architectural history and defined a new image of the city, still characterized today by horrible open spaces and by excessively wide roads. The areas that were preserved following the war are protected by UNESCO as part of humanity's cultural heritage. The question of how new building regulations can help reveal again the old structure of the city has been an important topic of debate since 1989.

The site addressed by the competition, intended for the "Wilhelmgalerie" office building and retail premises, is located on the north side of the Wilhelmplatz, a more or less rectangular square in the center of the city. Before the war the magnificent Gontard building, dating from 1767, stood here. The competition task was to re-establish in the square, by means of new building work, the spatial relationships which are only partly recognizable due to war damage and reconstruction, and to reclaim this space for civic use. The building was also to serve as an organizing element of the adjoining urban spaces.

It is clear that, given his way of understanding architecture, Dominique Perrault did not look to nostalgic reconstruction as the means of relating the location to its past, but instead proposed a new strategy. He was the only competitor who stepped back from the given site and offered a fresh interpretation of the square as a whole. In his project Perrault follows the

Editor of *Bauwelt* since 1990, and author of several books about contemporary architecture in Berlin and Paris.
He studied architecture in Braunschweig and Rome and practiced in several offices in Munich and Berlin.

monumental arrangement of the façades, which used to – and still do in part – characterize the location, but he does this only in a general way. For that reason he chose an architectural language which has nothing historicist about it and which forms the obvious sign of a new beginning. The project consists of two long buildings of equal width which, proceeding from the northernmost part of the site, occupy the east and west sides of the square. The streets skirting the square would, then, be built on either side. Various shops and cafés – freely distributed around the ground floor like large boxes – are found beneath rows of tall pillars that gaze up at the sky. Only above, on the slim cylindrical pillars, does a two-story built strip with offices appear: a kind of attic running along the whole building. Access to these floors is effected by means of glass elevators and staircases, while the roof is defined by extended bands of solar panels.

The rationale of this project is founded on a clear and obvious idea: for Perrault, urban life in the Wilhelmplatz stood in the foreground: a conjunction of relationships which could not be arrived at if the square were to be built up with a new enclosed city block. Thanks to the system of pillars and the open and flexible layout of the ground-floor shops and cafés, his design offers, furthermore, an open view of the entire square, with its lawn and rows of ancient trees. Perrault does not consider his two arcades as spaces hidden away within a city block but as open galleries which embrace the whole space of the square, to the benefit of the passers-by. The language of the façades uninhibitedly points up the lightness of the steel and glass architecture, and manages to fully integrate itself into the space of the square, despite its overall geometry being at odds with the setting. Even Potsdam needs an architecture that is forceful and innovatory, and which can thereby calmly compete with its historical buildings; a new identity certainly daring in its consequences, but which ought to be seen as the opportunity for a genuine new beginning.

Kansai-Kan Library

Kyoto, Seika-cho, 1996

THREE GARDENS FOR THE LIBRARY

THE NATURAL GARDEN   Once upon a time there was Nature, before Men cleared it and established their towns there. Today Man is in search of that part of himself he once believed he could do without. A bit of nature as a place to live, what could be more "natural" for a large library?

A vast wooden esplanade forms a wide drive; it is bordered by pines planted on a carpet of moss and well-mown grass. The trees, whose contours are to be shaped over the years, will create a foliate skyline fixed at the same height as the projecting glass of the library.

THE GLASS GARDEN   All but nothing, just a flash of light, a scintillating line: such is the immaterial and poetic sign of the Library's presence.

A sheet of glass with its changing reflections that irresistibly attract the eye. You make your way towards this "crystal" and enter a garden of glass. A huge kaleidoscope or telescope lens, the views are multiplied and intersected to infinity, blending the surrounding nature with the serene world of the reading rooms. This filter protects the library, tactfully covers it. This is the entrance, the reception area, the meeting place, the interface between inside and out.

THE READING GARDEN   At the heart of the library a huge space bathed in gentle, diffused overhead light accommodates and subsumes the various functions related to reading. As if in a garden, you discover small box-like constructions wrapped in fabric. Absorbing the sound, these "objects" delimit the calm and human-size reading areas. The light in this world is indirect and all movement silent.

FOUR ORGANIZATIONAL PLANS

THE READERS   The readers are at the center of the library, at the heart of the book-issuing system and right beside the librarians.

In this huge room, the arrangement is flexible to suit the needs of the readers, the scientific evolution of the collections and any technological transformations in ways of reading.

THE PERSONNEL   The librarians and their services surround the reading areas. This ring, or belt, constitutes the interface between the large reading room (communication) and the book stacks (conservation).

THE BOOKS   The books are distributed around the edges of the reading rooms; since there is no natural light, they are protected from the "outside world." The organization of the stacks is highly compact, in order to reduce the distance and the time of transport.

THE FUTURE EXTENSION   The extension follows the form of the ground. The nature garden is prolonged as far as the hill and the basement book storage areas follow the unfolding of the landscape. The extension can be undertaken in several stages. Its organisation is the geometrical continuation of the first phase.   **DP, 1996**

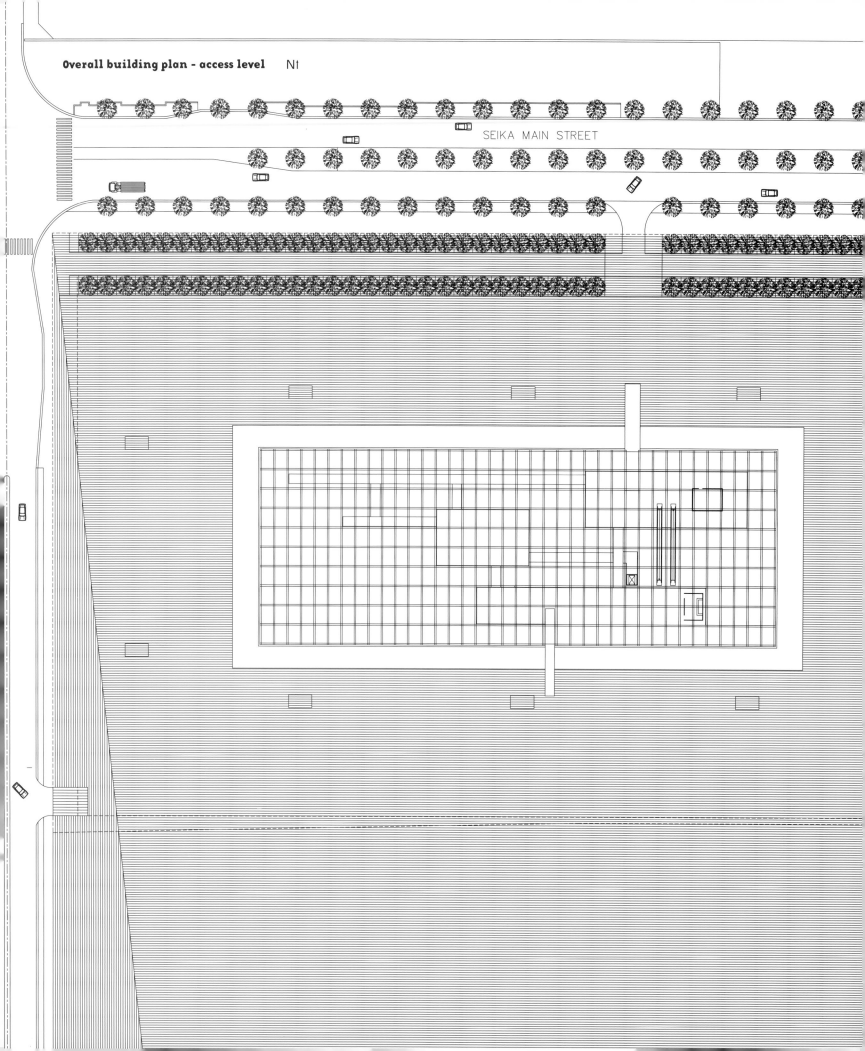

SEIKA MAIN STREET

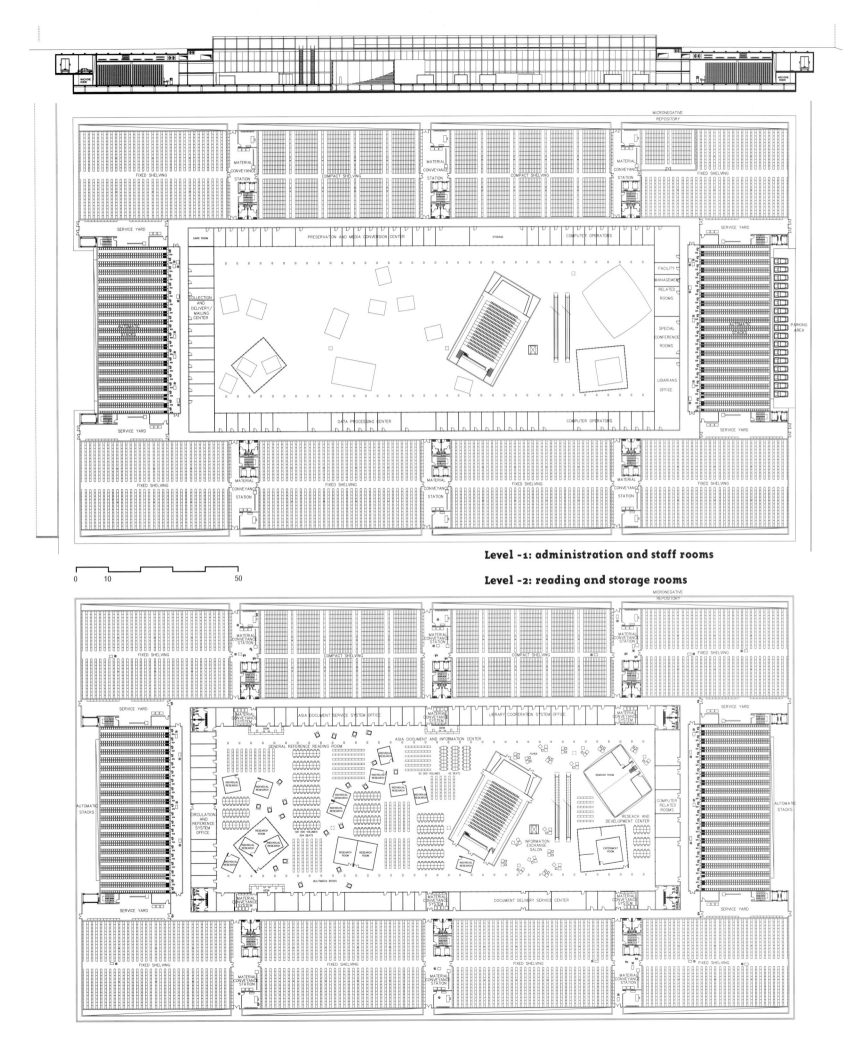

Level -1: administration and staff rooms

Level -2: reading and storage rooms

0   10   50

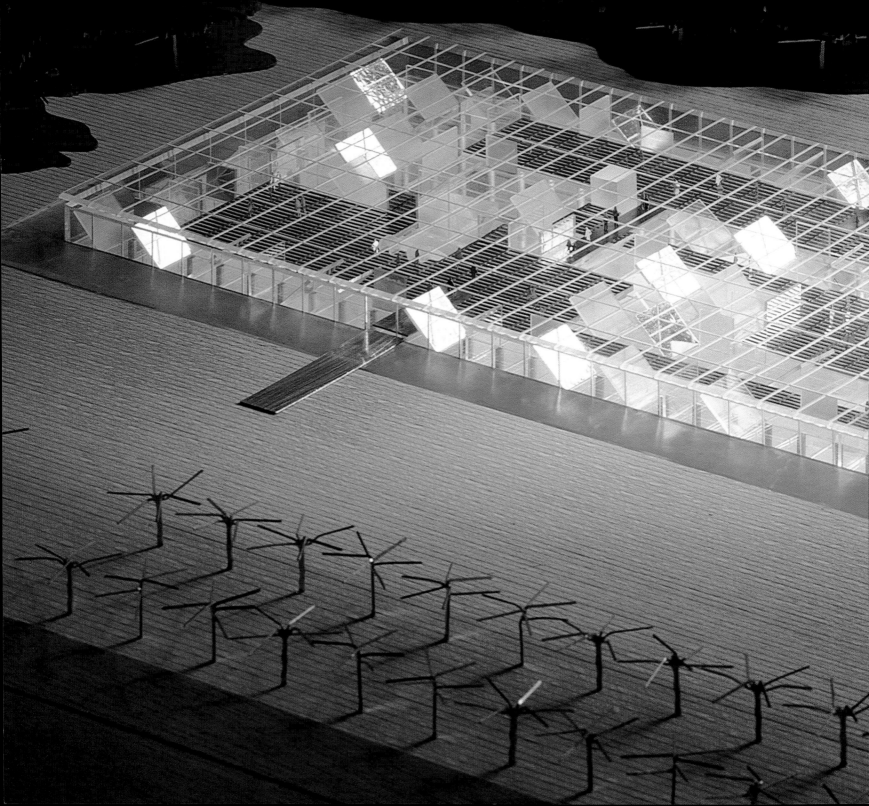

Botond Bognar

The concept of nature underlying the Japanese world view is by no means a reflection of nature in its original state. It is based on a landscape that has been carefully cultivated since prehistoric times. The countryside as a whole developed along with Japanese civilization, and Japan's cities represent the climax of that development....[T]he beautiful Japanese countryside is the result of our ancestors' unremitting care over 2,000 years; it is a far cry from nature in its unaltered state.   Noboru Kawazoe [1]

Crystal Garden   The planned Library, called in short Kansai-kan, would be located in the Kansai Science City, a new urban development not far south of Kyoto City, but equally close to Nara and Osaka.[2] Thus the site is rich in both the heritage of traditional Japanese culture and the pioneering spirit of the rapidly developing 21st century information society in Japan that now unmistakably shapes the progress of the country's urbanization, well manifested by not only metropolitan Osaka, but also Kyoto.[3]

Yet, outside of large urban centers, the area is endowed with nature in its unspoiled beauty and variety assured here by lush green hills and valleys that alternate with small fields and rice paddies. Many of the already completed buildings – residential areas, research facilities for telecommunication and information technology and other high-tech centers, such as the Keihanna Plaza Cultural Center, the International Institute for Advanced Studies, and especially the Research Institute of Innovative Technology for the Earth (RITE) – have been designed so as to preserve the environment as much as possible.[4]

Apparently the goal in Kansai Science City is to search for ways of arriving at a harmonious relationship or coexistence between the workings of advanced technologies and nature, and thus, between architecture and the environment, both past and future. Perrault's proposal for the new Library has been strongly guided by a similar ambition; the central idea of his scheme is a highly innovative contemporary, perhaps even futuristic, reinterpretation of the Japanese garden, which itself is, as it has always been, the artistic and sometimes highly abstract recreation of nature, and a place of contemplation.[5]

In order to preserve the natural landscape Perrault has designed most of the library as an underground facility. As in the case of an iceberg, only a small part, the entrance hall, reception area and lounge are above ground; altogether they are shaped as an extensive, one-story rectangular volume made entirely of structural glass. Perrault calls this part of his library a "glass garden." Yet, this "garden" is not merely a large glass box (120 x 48 x 3.6 m); inside it features a small "forest" of glass panels of various light-transmitting qualities: some are transparent, but most are opaque, polarizing translucent, and mirror glass.

In addition to the vertical ones, there are numerous inclined or slanting panels between the flat glass roof and the mostly glass floor, all of which reflect the light downwards in varying

Professor of architecture at the University of Illinois, he is a scholar of both traditional and contemporary Japanese architecture and urbanism. His book *Togo Murano: Master Architect of Japan* (1996) was the winner of a 1997 AIA International Book Award. He is currently working on his next book *Nikken Sikkei 1900-2000: Building Future Japan.*

ways, while also acting as solar control shading.[6] This entire assemblage of glass elements adds up to what seems to be a large prism or crystal laid over the wide-stretching green landscape, which it either reflects or, through its transparent surfaces, reveals; in other words, this glass garden, akin to a mirage, is both there and not there. From a distance its presence is revealed only when parts of its glass surface momentarily mirror the glow of the sky or bounce back the sun with a brilliant flash.

As one can imagine, the sight can be quite magical, yet the experience is further enhanced when one enters the space. Similar to being inside a huge kaleidoscope or, as in *Alice in Wonderland*,[7] here – again not unlike in traditional Japanese gardens – reality and illusion are inseparably merged.[8] While the surrounding nature is retained and, visually at least, continued inside, it is also shattered and rendered as a collage of shifting reflections that change with the direction and intensity of ambient light, and along one's movement through the space. The shallow pool around the rectangular, transparent glass volume reintroduces nature, both in its concrete material reality and as a reversed image; that is, as a fictive world beneath the surface of the water.

The actual library is, of course, also below this surface, underground. The huge compound is centered around the vast, three-story (10.8-meter-high) reading area arranged directly below the entrance space. The glassy structure therefore acts not only as a "typical" Japanese in-between space (*engawa*) mediating between outside and inside, or between the natural and man-made worlds, but – with its large-span steel lattice trusses – also as the roof structure, and, more importantly, as an enormous system of glass screens filtering and directing light down into this central part, the heart of Perrault's architecture.

This space below – the "reading garden," in Perrault's words – although activated by the spectacular lightshow from above, is recessed in the quieter, calmer underground realm and is more inward-focussed.[9] Sound is reduced by the interior arrangement and the chosen materials, which engender an altogether softer atmosphere than the one above.

The cavernous space – unified by the extensive glass ceiling above and also by the attenuated spectrum of light – is 'broken up' by the individual volumes of supporting functions related to reading and research. Wrapped in cloth, these sound-absorbing "objects" on the lowest level seem to "float" within their larger enclosure in a random manner. In this realm, the arrangement of furniture and fittings is flexible and can be adapted to the changing needs of the library.

The librarians' rooms, administrative offices, research rooms, lounges, and other service facilities surround the reading space on three levels while sharing its views and the light channeled through it. The vast system of stocks, or the storage areas of books in several fireproof blocks, on the other hand, are organized beyond this zone, at the peripheries of the complex, which are completely buried under the landscaped, natural garden stretching above. Future extension of the library storage is also planned to be underground.

The overall solution proposed for the Kansai-kan can be better understood – and thus also discussed – in reference to Perrault's opus magnum, the Bibliothèque nationale de France in Paris (1992-95). The Kansai library reinterprets the idea of the large sunken courtyard of its predecessor in Paris, but instead of providing an open area with planted trees or other vegetation, it does so in the extensive and fully covered space with the unique introduction of ambient light. In that sense, Perrault's design may reveal a dimension that is common with Tadao Ando's architecture – wherein nature is often captured through the poetic effect of light and shadow – but Perrault goes a step further, perhaps.

Whilst in the sunken reading areas, one at first may miss the direct views or the presence of the surrounding lush landscape and nature, but it will soon be discovered that their views, as in a curious, enchanted periscope, are actually provided through the large mirror-glass panels inclined at 45 degrees overhead, though transformed in the process of reflections. It might be said that in Perrault's design interventions Nature is prompted to emerge anew in a way that questions the "naturalness" of Nature itself, and understands it as a cultural phenomenon. This seems somewhat similar, if not identical, to the way Japanese culture has always reflected upon, or "(re)created" Nature, and which attitude is so eloquently explained by Noboru Kawazoe in the quote from him above.

The Kansai Library project once again proves, with poignancy, Perrault's unique design sensibilities; the fact that he – like a growing number of his contemporary designers, such as Toyo Ito, Tadao Ando, Fumihiko Maki, Yoshio Taniguchi, Norman Foster, Renzo Piano, Jean Nouvel, and many others in Japan and elsewhere – is capable of consistently putting forward a "new modernism" in architecture. Rejecting both the triviality of postmodernism and the rigid dogmas of modernism, and proposing innovative technological and design solutions, this architecture is not only sensitive to many environmental issues, but is also capable of enhancing that environment, natural or otherwise, as much as the human experience of it. Perrault himself put it this way: "...architecture, a seismograph for the culture of our human nature, forges our vision of the world and generates new emotions that are apprehended intuitively and not by the intellect."[10]

1 Noboru Kawazoe, "The Flower Culture of Edo," *Japan Echo* (special issue *Tokyo: Creative Chaos*) Vol.XIV (Tokyo, 1987):53.

2 The Kansai Science City is located about twenty five kilometers south of Kyoto within the triangular area defined by Kyoto, Nara, and Osaka; hence it is easily accessible from all three places.

3 Much of Japan's high-tech electronic and communications industry is located in or around Osaka and Kyoto, including the headquarters, factories, and research centers of such companies as Matsushita (National), Sharp, Sanyo, Kyocera.

4 Many of these structures, designed by the Japanese firm Nikken Sekkei, in addition to providing and/or preserving much of the greenery around them in the form of attractive gardens and parks, utilize various modes of energy-saving technologies. This is especially evident in the case of the Research Institute of Innovative Technology for the Earth (RITE) of 1993. Here Nikken Sekkei designers extensively used solar energy, natural ventilation, and water purification systems. As a matter of fact, the Institute itself is, as its name reveals, a place where these new environmental technologies are elaborated and tested.

5 The famous dry or stone gardens of Japan, including the ones at Ryoan-ji (1490s) and Daitoku-ji (1509) Zen Temples in Kyoto are the most abstract or transcendental, and certainly the most evocative recreations of not only nature as such, but also the world or Reality itself.

6 The entrance hall floor is a mixture of glass and metal panels. Metal panels are used where the main circulation areas are located. The outside bridges crossing the reflective pool to the entrances are also shaped with highly polished metal plates, so that visitors may have the impression that they are walking on water.

7 This is a reference to Lewis Carroll, *Alice's Adventures in Wonderland*.

8 Japanese gardens, even the most natural-looking gardens for walking in (*kaiyushiki-niwa*), were entirely artificially created, and employed numerous artistic techniques to challenge human imagination and appear more than they were in reality. Their highly sophisticated episodic ("kaleidoscopic") arrangement always allows for different ways of mentally recreating their totality (of experience), which remains necessarily elusive. For further details see Teiji Itoh, *Space and Illusion in the Japanese Garden* (Tokyo: Weatherhill, 1973).

9 Quoted from Dominique Perrault's project description (1996).

10 Dominique Perrault, "Foreword" in *Dominique Perrault, Des Natures - Beyond Architecture* (Basel, Boston, Berlin: Birkhäuser Verlag, 1996):8.

Kolonihavehus
Installation

"A house, a tree," and an enclosure: this is the Kolonihaven typology. Nature "of one's own," a bit of ground "of one's own" and a house that expresses the inhabitant's sensibility. Expressive, gay, exotic...but above all unique. This tiny territory with its tree is a treasure. It opens onto the environment in order to assert itself and thereby "live together." An enclosure of four sheets of glass stake their claim. This glass box harnesses nature, which is then possessed and shared by man... The real nature of our nature; what other nature is there? **DP**, 1996

255

Town Hall

Rolf Reichert

When, in the spring of 1996, the town of Innsbruck invited him to participate in an international competition for the Town Hall Passage, Dominique Perrault suggested we collaborate with him in the realization of the project. Thanks to the confidence gained as a consequence of our extended participation on the Berlin Olympic cycle track and swimming pool, and due to his experience of the thought processes and work methods of the Germans – acquired on the Salzburg and Munich competitions, among others – he was sure, right from the start, that for this difficult project in the town center it was vital to have a collaborator who spoke German.

In a project as complex and important for the town of Innsbruck as this one, not only do the urbanistic and formal aspects play an important role, but the political ones do, too. For that reason an exact understanding of the parameters within which a project like this one may become possible is essential. Along with a knowledge of the German language, it is essential to sense, understand, and correctly apply the way of thinking of the sponsors of the competition, and the political environment. Not having taken these factors into account is, among others, the reason why most entries, especially the foreing ones – with the exception of Guido Canali's – were completely mistaken, in my opinion and also in the opinion of the jury.

During the preparatory phase of the competition, which took place concurrently in Paris and Munich – first by fax, then by e-mail –, the sketches originating in Paris were continually being screened and adapted to what was feasible and justifiable within the framework of the complex preexisting factors. Dominique meant for the design to be not only spectacular, as the Munich one had been, but also for it to respect, echo and complement the characteristics of the site. For our part, we were hoping to endow this area of the town with a new urban entitity which was recognizable and up-to-date, although modest in size. We therefore proposed a town hall with a tower and balcony with which the town could easily identify itself.

Unfortunately the private investors considered that the part corresponding to the retail area did not adequately fulfil their expectations, and so the jury called for a second phase of the competition, restricted to our team and that of Guido Canali. Regrettably, a restructuring of the private investment involved paralysed all deliberation for a year and a half.

In January 1998 the jury met again and decided, unanimously this time, to select our project alone for future development. According to the jury, it was the one which responded most satisfactorily to the urbanistic, formal and functional demands of the program, within the confines of which the requirements of commercial exploitation were also adequately fulfilled.

Architect, partner at Atelier Reichert-Pranschke-Maluche Architekten, Munich. He is member of the Urban Planning Commission of Munich and Co-Director of the Institute of Architects of Bavaria. Since 1993, he has been an associate of Dominique Perrault for the construction of the Olympic velodrome and swimming pools in Berlin.

261

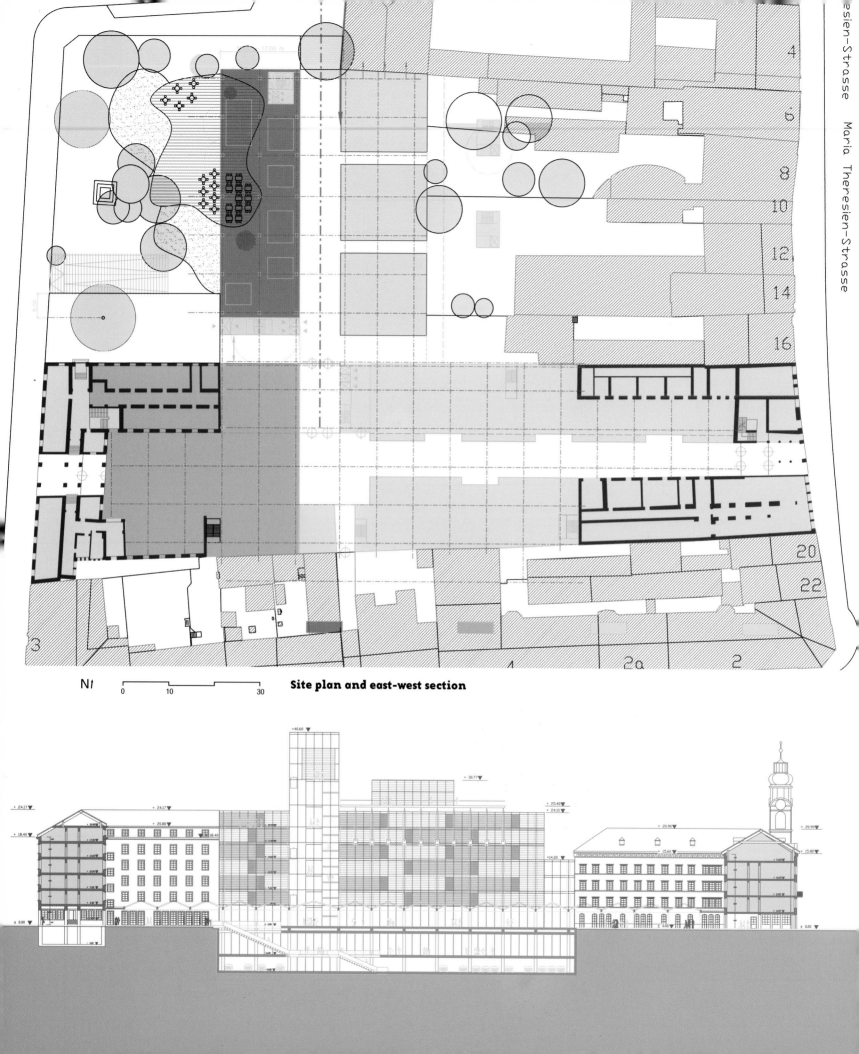

17.00 m

5.00

4

6

8

10

12

14

16

20

22

3

4

2a

2

N↑

0   10   30

Site plan and east-west section

+40.60

+30.77

+25.40
+24.10

+24.17   +24.17   +25.90   +25.90

+20.80   +15.60   +15.90

+18.40   +16.40   +14.20

+ 0.00   ± 0.00   ± 0.00

The Museum of Modern Art

The work presented here constitutes an open-ended architectural investigation. It is not a catalog of projects: instead, proceeding from an analysis of context, we establish a diagnosis which presents different potential responses. The interest this diagnosis has resides, on the one hand, in the identification of elements to be protected, and on the other, in that of the elements to be designed and projected. The first form the system's common trunk; the rest constitute the Museum's developments and metamorphoses.

Urban analysis shows the difference in nature and function between 53rd and 54th Streets: one is more pedestrian-oriented. This opposition constitutes a specific urban feature of the MoMA: street (53rd) side and garden (54th) side. This reading of the site clarifies the urban situation by dividing, lengthwise, the block – built on 53rd Street – open towards 54th.

It cannot, though, be said that there is a "front" and a "back," but rather a streetside Museum and a gardenside Museum.

The organizational structure of the MoMA could be compared to a "tree." It digs down into the earth as if searching its "life force" there. In an opposed movement, it thrusts a long built mass emphatically upwards to form its "trunk." Then, blossoming out, it extends its branching structure – its "treetop" – aside, above and along. Crowning the whole thing, the tower soars up into the sky, where it participates in the aerial concert of its no less prestigious neighbors.

Since we were evoking roots and branches, it is fitting, firstly, to elaborate a trunk. This element forms the core of the project. Architectural and functional analysis of the existing building shows that the exhibition rooms do not have their place, or more precisely their "correct place," there. By freeing the floors currently given over to exhibitions, and by moving the library and conservation departments there, we put the existing building to better use as regards its organization and the quality of its work spaces. The enlarged and more ventilated offices occupy the upper part of the building and all benefit from natural light.

Forming part of the same undertaking, the extension of the garden hall to the whole of the building (length- and height-wise) creates a place full of life and movement, bathed in natural light, with all levels being served by a set of vertical and horizontal circulations.

By following, developing and amplifying the morphology of the existing building, the Trunk, the life-giving element of the MoMA, is thus formed.

Starting from the trunk, three potential positions for the museum exhibition rooms can be imagined: aside, along and above it. **DP, 1997**

Terence Riley

The New Museum of Modern Art [1]   Since 1939, when The Museum of Modern Art (MoMA) was first able to commission a building of its own, the goal of the institution has been not only to provide functional space, but to express its "understanding of modern art in concrete form." As we now approach a new century, the Museum must meet unique challenges in presenting the arts of our time while remaining attuned to dual considerations: the need for additional space for the growing collection, as well as the quality of that space. Twice in the past the Museum relied on Trustees to design its buildings: Philip L. Goodwin and Philip Johnson. Goodwin (with Edward Durell Stone) designed the first building, and Johnson designed all but one of its subsequent additions. For the current expansion, the Museum invited Wiel Arets, Jacques Herzog and Pierre de Meuron, Steven Holl, Toyo Ito, Rem Koolhaas, Dominique Perrault, Yoshio Taniguchi, Bernard Tschumi, Rafael Viñoly, and Tod Williams and Billie Tsien to participate in a charette, a problem-solving design exercise. The charette participants met in January 1997 at the Museum to familiarize themselves with its urban, spatial, and physical characteristics, as well as to engage in a dialogue with the trustees, chief curators, and senior staff about the conceptual and programmatic nature of the new Museum.

The participants were asked to consider the nature and range of options for planning the new Museum and to document their thinking in both written and graphic form. The essence of the design exercise was the exploration of basic urbanistic and conceptual strategies for the redevelopment of the entire Museum. As the Charette was not a formal design competition, the architects were not asked to develop, refine, and present a single, optimized scheme. Rather, the goal was to generate multiple responses to the site conditions and to the Museum's preliminary conceptual and programmatic needs. Dominique Perrault's investigations focused on the grand urban gesture,

Chief Curator of Architecture and Design at The Museum of Modern Art, New York. He studied architecture at the University of Notre Dame and Columbia University and before joining the Museum established an architectural practice with John Keenen. Keenen/Riley's work has been published and exhibited widely.

the search for an overall parti diagram that would best represent a reconstructed Museum. All of the architect's explorations derive from an analysis of the Museum's public space using a tree as a metaphor, the trunk representing the principal circulation spaces and the branches and sub-branches representing the myriad of different destinations within the Museum. As did a number of architects, Perrault projected a central "spine" of public spaces and circulation dividing the site and running in an east-to-west direction. Based on this metaphorical conception, the architect projected three partis, which he described as "Aside," "Along," and "Above." The first concentrates the new construction principally on the site of the existing Dorset Hotel — whose addition extends the Museum's ground plan far to the west — treating the project more like an expanded wing of the Museum rather than a synthetic restructuring. The second proposal, "Along," projects a long, narrow extension of the Museum running the entire length of the site from east to west, with a reconfigured sculpture garden running parallel to it along Fifty-fourth Street. The final scheme, "Above," envisions a vast horizontal plane hovering above the existing and new sites at approximately the seventh-floor level; containing the gallery spaces, the scheme includes an open ground level that would provide for a greatly expanded sculpture garden. In essence, the organizational structure of the Museum would reflect the overall structure of the expanded Museum: a north-to-south striation and a vertical striation, in the "Along" and "Above" schemes, respectively. The diverse architectural and urban position of the Charette submissions succeeded in broadening the Museum's awareness of the complex issues involved in designing a museum for the twenty-first century in a dense urban environment, as well as the potential for exciting solutions.

1 Adapted with permission from *Studies in Modern Art 7: Imagining the Future of The Museum of Modern Art*, ©1998 by the Museum of Modern Art, New York.

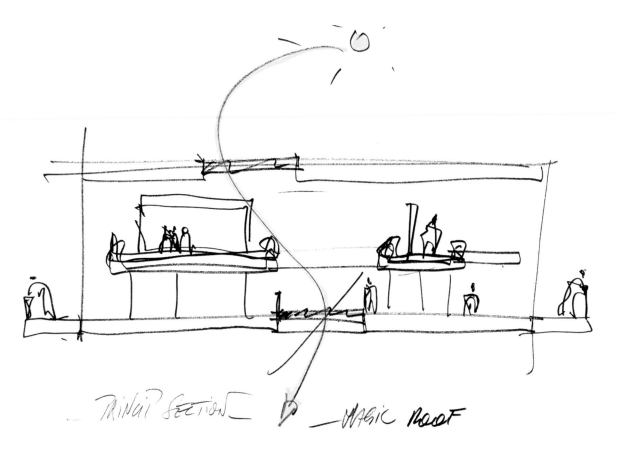

MAIN SECTION   _MAGIC ROOF_

ABOVE   In pursuing the investigation of an architectural expansion for the exhibition galleries from a single common trunk, another possibility emerges, the idea of building above:

A roof for human occupation, floating above the garden and covering the existing building.

A roof, like a huge thin leaf, unifying the diversity of the buildings – a shelter in the mythical sense of the original house, which protects the human group and its culture from the hostility of the world.

A roof bathed in light and air, permeable to light and water, allowing each to pass at certain places and permitting the garden to "breathe" according to its natural rhythm.

A roof between sky and earth, bordering 54th Street, without walling it off or shading it.

A roof crowning the 53rd Street buildings, defined as artists' studios that would form an extended glass attic.

A roof whose length offers a wide range of planning possibilities, a flexibility relating to the administration and growth of the collections.

A roof in which the museum tour is flexible and free.

A roof which gives the MoMA its identity as a cultural building, yet largely open to the public.

A roof in keeping with the sensibility and vision of contemporary art, like an "installation" that gives an "other" meaning to the site as a whole: a metamorphosis, or transfiguration even, of the place itself.

A roof lending identity to a site, while preserving the difference between its parts, like some reference to the notion of democracy described by Monsieur de Tocqueville.

A roof that causes us to fantasize about an architecture freed from gravitational pull – a certain idea of immateriality. **DP, 1997**

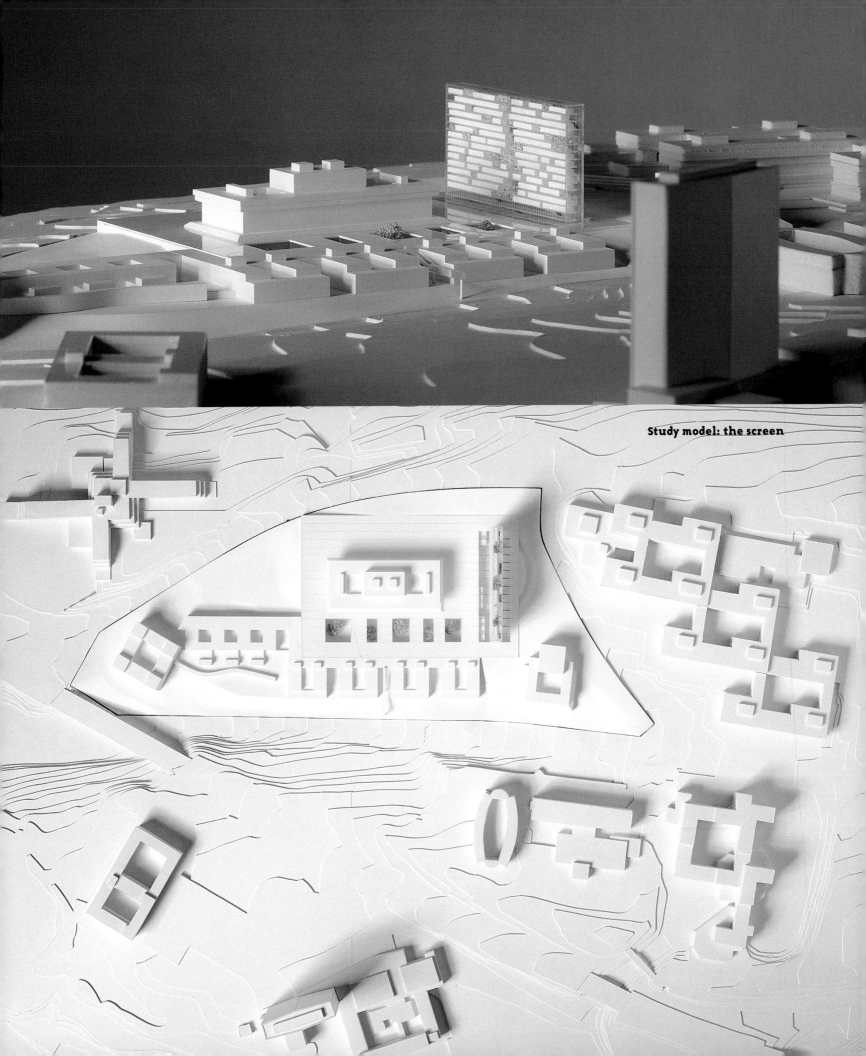

Study model: the screen

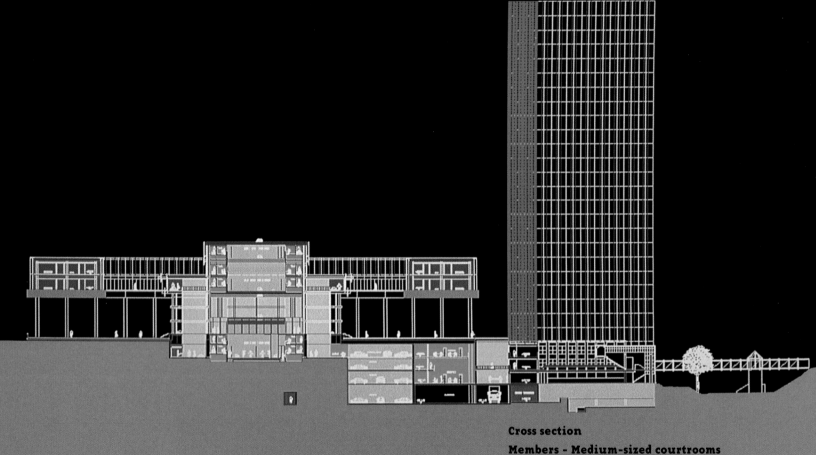

Cross section

Members - Medium-sized courtrooms
The peristyle - Ambulatory room

APLIX Factory
Nantes, Le Cellier, 1997-1999

The factory is meant for the production of "self-gripping systems" and synthetic fiber fabrics. Non-polluting for the environment, this activity is of interest to the community for the number of jobs it will create following its opening. Its potential for development will lend a certain dynamism to the region. On top of that, the design attempts to offer optimum working conditions and to guarantee a flexible integration of future extensions. This project, then, marks the beginning of an industrial change in the community.

We have placed an orthogonal 20 x 20m grid on top of the site, forming a checkerboard of metal and vegetal surfaces. The composition of the factory itself is the result of the juxtaposition of several 20 x 20m blocks, 7.7 m high. In the initial proposal, the form of the factory is that of a long, regularly stepped rectangle. The main façade gives onto the main RN23 road; windowless, it expresses the desire for interiorization linked to the architectural project and to the confidentiality of the activity of production with the strict design of a thin, extended line from which a few treetops protrude.

Running parallel to the RN23, the continuous and fluid space of an interior street which constitutes the building's true backbone allows for the circulation of fork-lift trucks and the intersection of the entire flow of raw materials and finished products. Three 20 x 40 m rectangular-based gardens covered with lofty plantations cling to the interior street; the russet bark and bluish foliage of pine trees, which will be 12 meters high at the end of construction work, provide them with a touch of color, while their airy tops allow the refracted light to enter the interior street. Around these gardens, and for each of the two divisions, the various workshops are organized according to the manufacturing cycle of the product.

The visible material is a slightly burnished metal sheeting. An idealized expression of agricultural buildings, it reflects the surrounding nature and allows the factory to gently blend into it. Each part of the project is conceived so as to enable the envisaging of workshop extensions and parking areas. For that reason, the rigorous conception of the composition's masses and their effects remains subject to variation. Extensions are possible via the aleatory articulation of supplementary squares, which would thus create visual irregularities, notably in the frontal view; for the moment, then, there is no definitive configuration of the extensions to the factory, but rather the wish for a game of chance elicited by the metal/vegetal encounter of volumes and reflections. **DP, 1998**

285

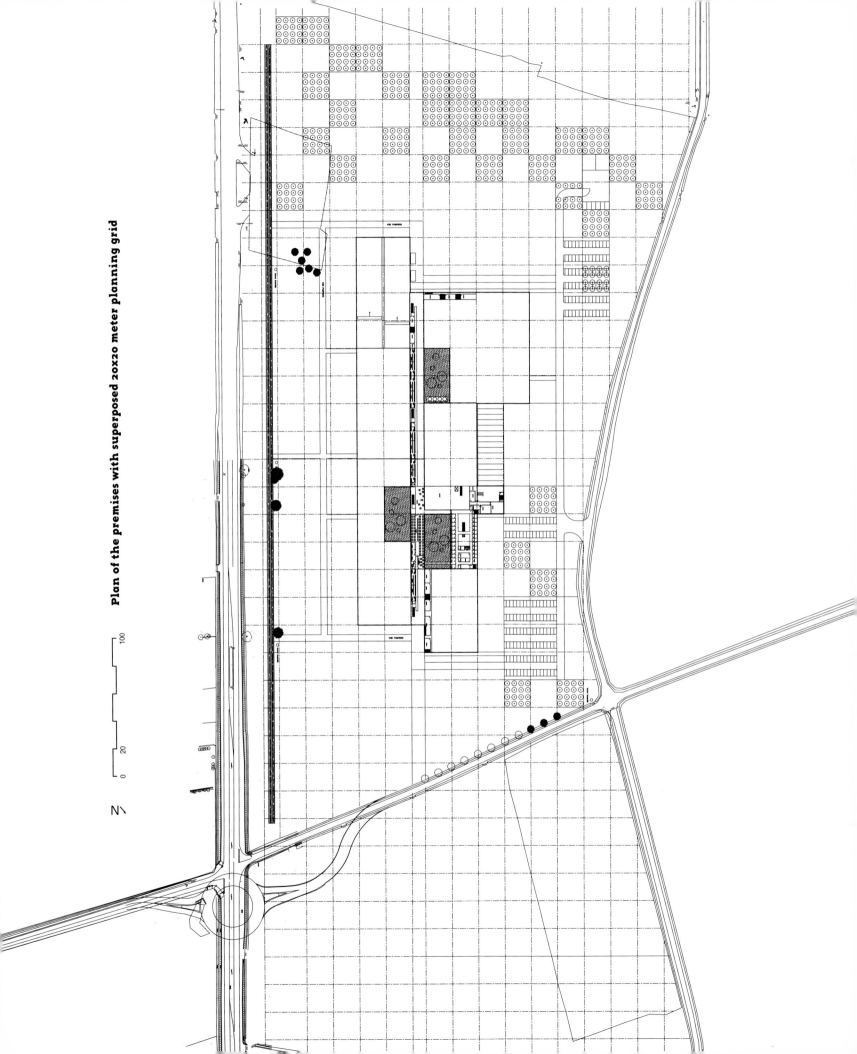

Plan of the premises with superposed 20x20 meter planning grid

Lehrter Bahnhof Tower

Berlin, 1998

The study of a high-rise building on the station square involves three sizes or scales: the public space of the square, the quality of the neighborhood and the city skyline. One understands the a priori interest in building a landmark building in the new station area, but is it necessary to, and must one plonk it right on the main square? This isn't a neighborhood on the edges of the city, which stands rejected. It's an interface between the territory of the Land (and the whole country) and that of the city. The presence of an architectural signifier or a collection of architectural signifiers constituting a specific local skyline combines to give it an identity, a particular character. Our task consists in liberating the space of the square in order to create a "real" station square, the widest and largest possible.

Three scenarios have been studied:

Scenario A – A TOWER BESIDE THE RIVER SPREE   If we pose the question of where best to build a tower in the central station area, our unequivocal reply is: beside the Spree, in front of the Tiergarten and the capital's government district. This site is worthy of the finest works of urban design, be they ancient, medieval or modern. The location is perfect for accommodating a "solitary," hence "unique," building. A tower, yes, but a tall, a very tall tower. A building visible from all over Berlin, an unforgettable construction set in a prestigious landscape. Rarely has there been, in Berlin, such an obvious site for a skyscraper. As we see it, such an unusual, special case deserved to be put on the agenda.

Scenario B – A TOWER ON THE FAR SIDE OF THE SQUARE   The positioning of a tower on the square, as its background and parallel to the basin, goes with and qualifies the entrance to the station concourse by disengaging, freeing and opening up the public space of the square to the surrounding town. From the point of view of the buildings situated between tower and basin, however, the proximity of the tower is strong. To build along the street, on either side of it, is a truly urban ambition. We seek to ratify this urban type without being detrimental to the neighboring buildings. The idea of a huge lobby at the foot of the tower provides an architectural response to this urban situation. The height of the lobby is equal to that of the neighboring blocks of flats, namely around 25-27 meters. This lobby is faced entirely in clear glass. The tower emerges above the line of the roof, and ends at a height of 160 meters.

Scenario C – A TOWER BETWEEN SQUARE AND CANAL BASIN   Pursuing the idea of opening up the space of the square to the maximum, we propose building nothing on the square itself but around it instead. To that end, and as an extension of the preceding idea, we have imagined emphasizing the station to the full with an urban square and opening up this square onto the neighborhood and, in particular, on to the basin. Acting as a light filter, the tower – a glass sheet situated between earth and water – frames the square and allows for views towards the basin. The advantage of this position for a high-rise building is obvious: uninterrupted views and generous setbacks in relation to its neighbors. The building itself is larger, organized on the proportions of the triangle of the station square. It is not as tall, the top of it reaching 144 meters.   **DP, 1998**

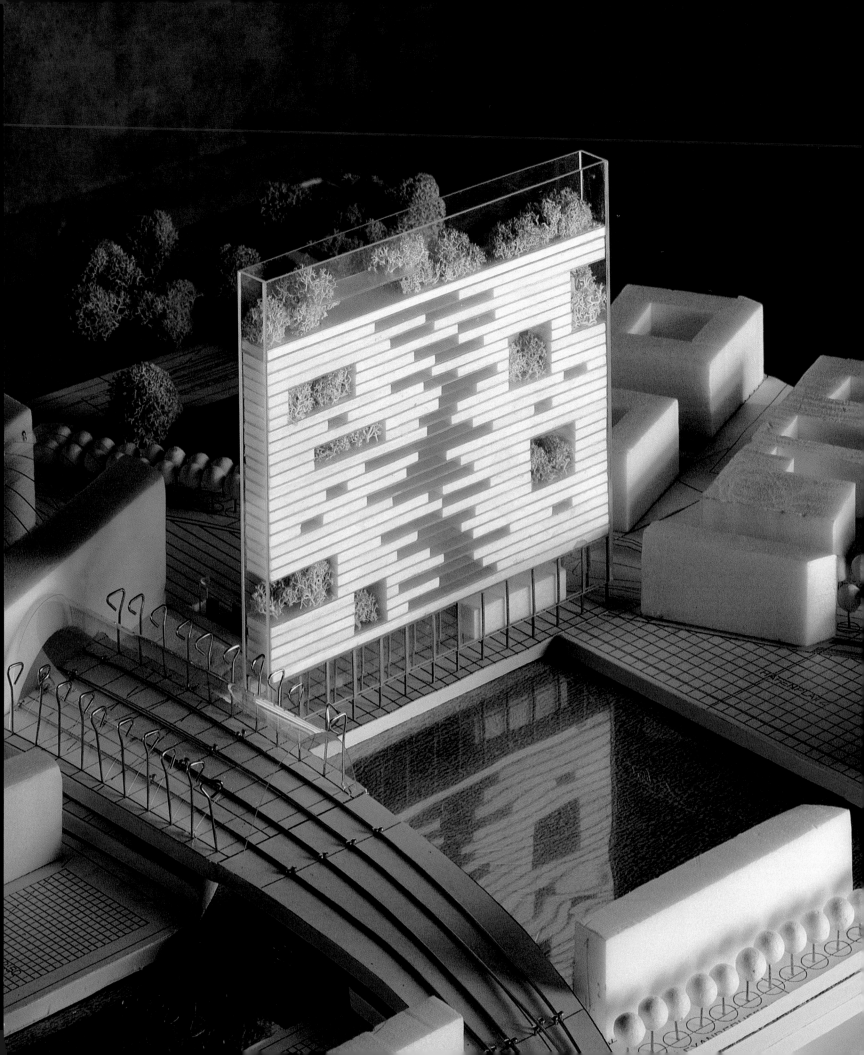

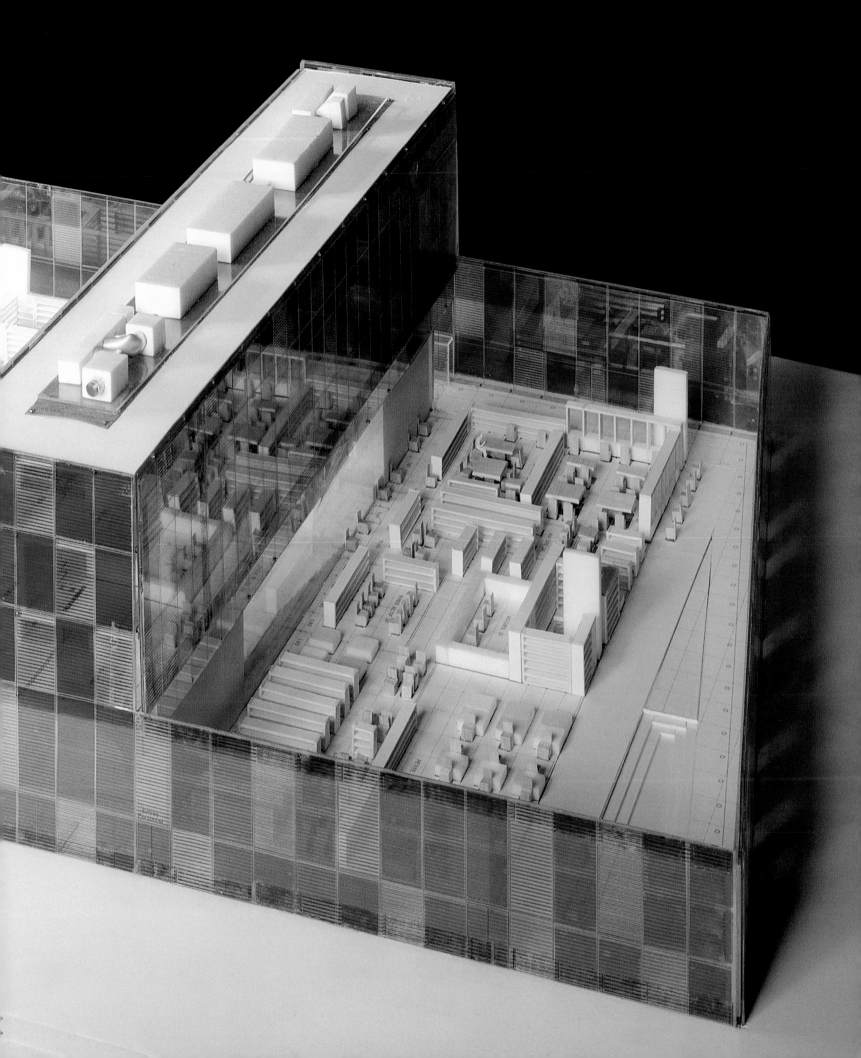

Bench for the WANAS Foundation

Gaëlle Lauriot-Prévost

FROM THE IRONY OF THE BED TO THE METAMORPHOSIS OF THE BENCH

What is it?

Is it a bed, is it a bench?

Whatever the answer, it is a mattress, a long, wide bit of bedding, a plump-looking cushion stretched out on a framework.

This framework, of soldered metal tubing, forms the basic structure of the object and seems to have a supporting role, somewhat along the lines of a mattress base.

Yet this mattress is boxed. It is covered, in fact, by a plexiglass envelope, forming a cavity protecting it.

The cushion idea no longer existing, it loses its mattress identity. In fact, this supposedly quilted element is not made of a supple stuff filled with a stuffing serving to comfortably support a part of the body: it is a box containing a mattress.

The whole thing gives the illusion of a bed, the image of a mattress, but its rigidity again alludes to the idea of the bench: here, it is transformed into a long, backless seat on which many people can sit at the same time.

This ordered superposition of different materials thus forms a horizontal couch, in both the real and figurative sense of the word.

So we ask ourselves then, feigning ignorance: is it a bed or is it a bench?

And the ironical reply is: it is a bench bed! In the same way that a bed can be a box bed, a divan bed, a folding bed, a cot bed, a portable bed, a camp bed...

Architect-designer, graduated from the École Camondo in Paris. She is art director of the office of Dominique Perrault, and co-author of the furniture for the Bibliothèque nationale de France.

Temple of Mithra

In the heart of Naples, the population density is greater than in Hong Kong.

In the heart of Naples, sedimentation of the layers of history has been effected
by the telluric alchemy of this area of the globe.

In the heart of Naples, the blood of men is mixed with the blood of volcanoes.

Noise, smell, heat, topography, movement are so many ingredients of a Neapolitan
character which only finds respite in the presence of an exuberant nature.

The Temple of Mithra, an open-air ruin stuck at the end of a canyon of over-inhabited
buildings, is a stopover in time. This mark in the ground, this imprint of History,
this trace of a flamboyant mythology, sizzles beneath the never-ending heat of the
Neapolitan city.

The design for a hanging garden, suspended between earth and sky as if torn from the
geological crust, offers a moment of calm and repose in this pullulating neighborhood.
Such a poetic and violent telluric gesture permits matter to be extricated from itself.

To emerge from its geological layer, let its entrails be glimpsed as if they were some
didactic section, thus showing that Naples is a deep city.

A bit of nature, floating free, raised on a terrace by a root-like bunch of metal pins:
such is this Garden of Babylon planted in the heart of the melted stone.

And so the temple appears below, empty, expressing its mystery without, for all that,
offering any explanation.

It will be necessary to penetrate inside, bury oneself there while discovering its
innermost recesses – which will be the sole indications of a slow and defunct history.

That is what this architectural project reveals by means of a geological section:
a place's history in the shape of Neapolitan ice cream. **DP, 1999**

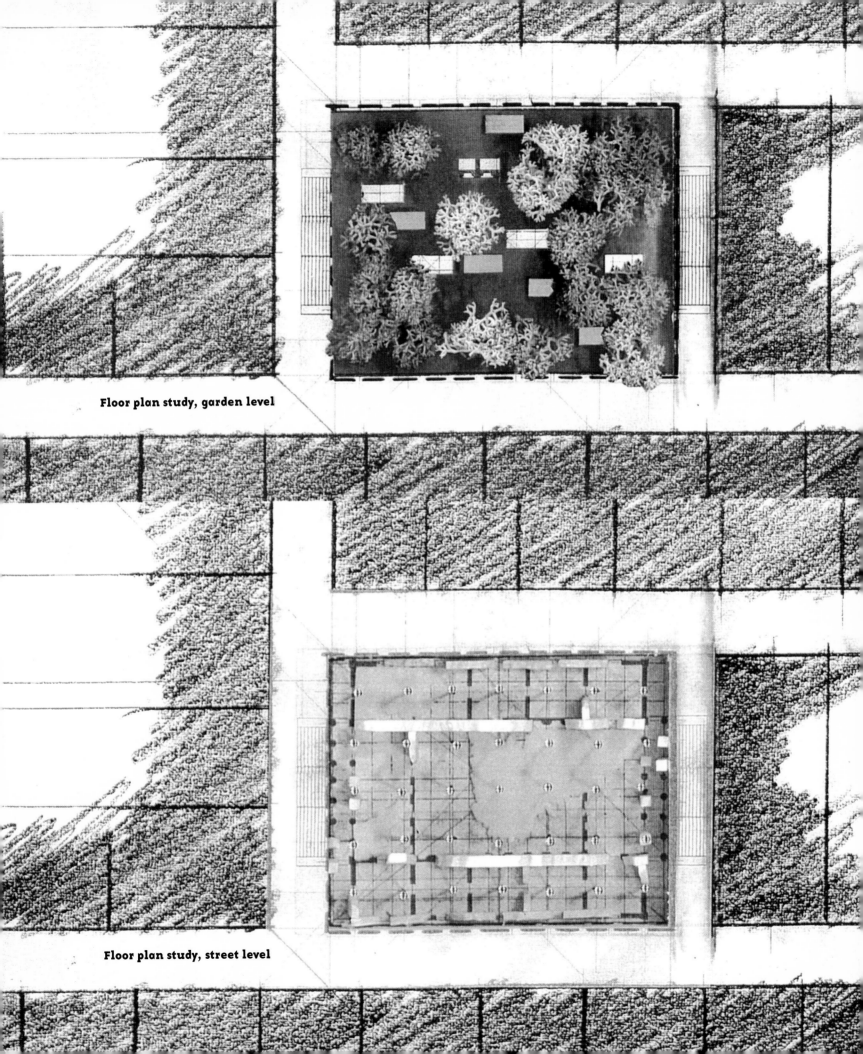

Floor plan study, garden level

Floor plan study, street level

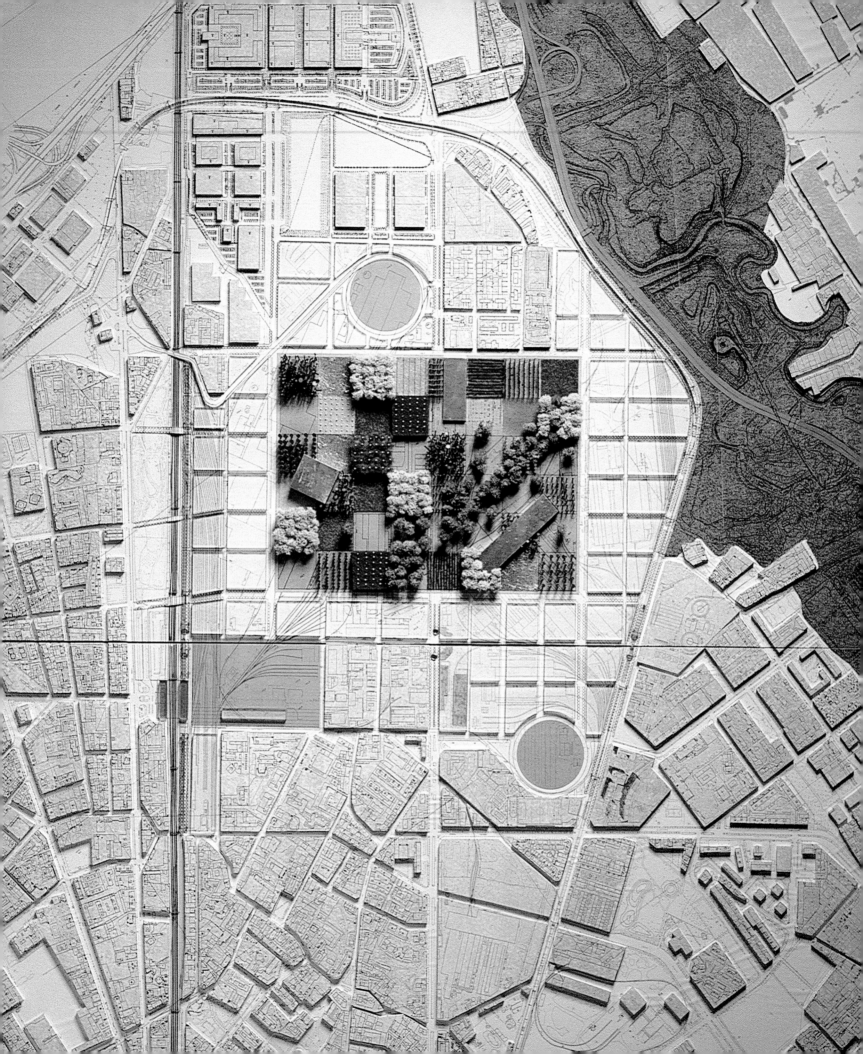

Redevelopment of the Falck site

To the north of Milan, on the remains of a huge industrial site, at the center of an emerging urban neighborhood, and along the edge of a long and winding planned "green corridor," it seemed right to create an adjoining "green space", half-urban, half-natural, and modern – that is, without reference to earlier centuries – linking order and disorder, rigor and fantasy, simplicity and exuberance.

The idea of the project is to give birth/semblance to a park at the heart of the town. That is to say, to develop the town and its streets, avenues, blocks, squares and gardens so as to reunite the southern neighborhoods with those in the north, the east with the west; in a word, TO WEAVE NEW LINKS / RELATIONS between the different districts. The natural layout of this park makes no reference to French-, Italian- or English-style gardens. This garden is an act of LAND ART, an act of contemporary art which considers the history of the site and its industrial context as a source of "building material" for conceiving a park specific to Sesto San Giovanni. Nature as a material forming the architecture of a town is not a new idea. But NATURE CONSIDERED AS AN INDUSTRIAL ELEMENT, as in the aeroplane, locomotive and other engine parts formerly manufactured in the Falck factories, that is something new, something rich in historical resonance, yet also up-to-date and even forward-looking.

This binary grid, akin to a chessboard – with its 95 x 95 m squares – permits the setting up of a supple, open and flexible system of realization. We will construct it square by square, respecting certain traces on the ground, or certain fine trees, or certain industrial buildings for their structure or their volume. It is necessary to "give time to time." Step by step, square after square, the town is built, the park laid out. With no aesthetic a priori as to style, just a basic geometry, measure and reading so as NOT TO LOSE ANYTHING of the existing context, WHILE TRANSFORMING IT INTO A NEW BIT OF TOWN, rich in urban diversity. **DP, 1998**

de France is that there are no walls to help define its identity. Something akin to lived experience must give shape to this building, the unity of an understanding that privileges individual discovery, personal experience. For a program devoted to learning, to knowledge, this is a kind of homage which, in denying the academic representation of a truth, emphasizes an understanding of learning as a discovery. The Bibliothèque nationale de France is not what is visible, and when we experience it, it appears different, it evokes an idea of discovery which is generic to what a library should be. We do not come out of a library the same way we went in; we do not come out of a library untouched. You are not meant to come out of this building untouched, either.

The extremely poignant spatial experiences, the encounter with a place, the fleeting idea of a building, this extremely brief and ephemeral moment – all ultimately have a very minor part to play in the realization process. I want to re-evaluate and reveal this somewhat brief encounter which conditions the choices that guide a project, the feeling of having identified something, an equilibrium which, while it may be called into question, changed, constitutes a privileged moment. Through the creation and placing of a certain number of objects one positions architecture within the territory, establishes an architectural concept which seeks to escape the plan, the traditional unfolding, of the project; this becomes almost a battle in which objects must be arranged and not drawn on a plan. The plan, as it is understood in architecture, is largely insufficient. It can only represent things and function within an overly linear system. To encapsulate a building in a design is very reductive. The plan is only a medium, a conceptual procedure that must not be overestimated. The design methodology must be thus subverted. In the initial, more conceptual, phase there is a sort of zero degree of intervention; this is the shortest phase in time terms. Next, there is the phase of elaborating the project, which brings in the tactile dimension, sensuality, the material. These two dimensions do not, in my opinion, emerge at the same moment; the concept cannot restrict the phenomenal aspect to being a simple abstraction. In my work, instead, these highly determined, box-like

buildings are a sort of dissertation on the box, remain as unfinished buildings.
They are permeable, permissive, and are open to transformation from the people
who use and inhabit them, who live inside them and can change their nature.
The concept can no longer be the phase prior to the project, that idealized moment
which presupposes that the architecture is a mere application of the concept.
The constructed architectural object is not an accomplishment, the definitive
manifestation of a creation. We must shake up this ideology of a unilateral expertise,
of the architect's specific knowledge. Architecture has no one truth. Architecture
exists in act, I take it as the work of an architect who, according to differing
paradoxical situations, creates living objects which adapt to human measure,
to the finitude of the human. Albeit highly defined, my buildings are open works.
The very nature of the architectural object must change, we have to oblige ourselves
to refuse an architecture whose procedures are cumbersome, and a practice which
remains within the realms of representation.

If we look only as far as the rules of the discipline, if we go on seeking to use a finite, closed language, the danger arises of a break with the public.

It is essential to leave the traditional field of architecture behind, to extend it to other domains in order to go beyond constituted language, to proceed by graftings, by artificial insemination. Without demand, architecture — based on reality principles — does not exist, it must be operational. DP, 1998

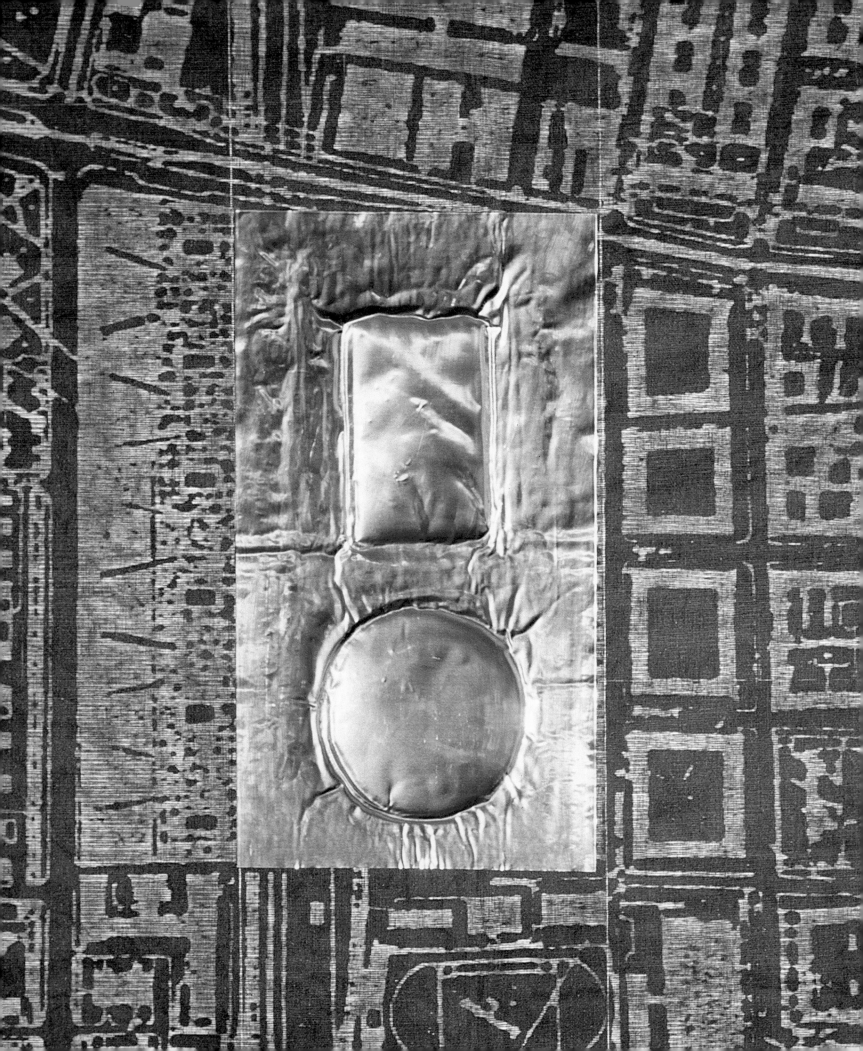

around a classical principle: a plinth, above which rises the monument represented by the four towers. Likewise, Berlin resembles a plinth awaiting its statue; yet such a crowning monument will never arrive. The design appears to be limited to the establishment of a substructure, and its implementation to altimetric adjustments for reducing the incision formed at street-level, an incision resulting from the principle of burial. This absence of materialization, and the lack of expression which results from it, encourages the idea that the architecture is no longer an end, but a means. There is no longer an apotheosis to organize, but a stage to set above the city. As if, after the formal excesses form of Le Corbusier and the asceticism of Mies, one was arriving at an almost non-existent architecture mobilizing the site around a gap which reveals the vacuity of contemporary life. Aside from its very materiality, the plinth addresses the nothingness created by the hurly-burly of recent urbanization. This stage articulates Perrault's urban conception, one that considers the urban fabric not in terms of morphology but as a texture perceived as a retinal phenomenon, almost as a still-life consisting of found objects and disparate constructions. Conceived as an optical device, the project comes up against the limits of such a strategy, because the town only gives back the image of its contingent reality – and Berlin's image today is hardly a glittering one.

In the second place, the Berlin sports complex is reduced to the characteristics of the metal skin that uniformly covers it. Artificially high-tech, the construction, defined by openly modern techniques, has neither performance nor bravura as its goal. It aspires to expressing nothing other than its own times. Perrault, in fact, grants little importance to the structure, thus repudiating the tradition of structural rationalism developed by Auguste Perret and his idea of a sovereign shelter in which load distribution is treated in a dramatic manner. Perrault's approach to the envelope and its texture brings him closer to Gottfried Semper, in the importance accorded to the weave. Actually, the swimming pool and velodrome only exist by dint of the homogeneous metal lattice which serves as a facing for the walls. The attention lavished on this skin grows out of a refined, even delicate, work in which an outpouring of feelings, along with notions of tactile pleasure, rediscovers its rights. "All, there, is order and beauty. Extravagance, calm and sensual delight," Baudelaire would perhaps have conceded.

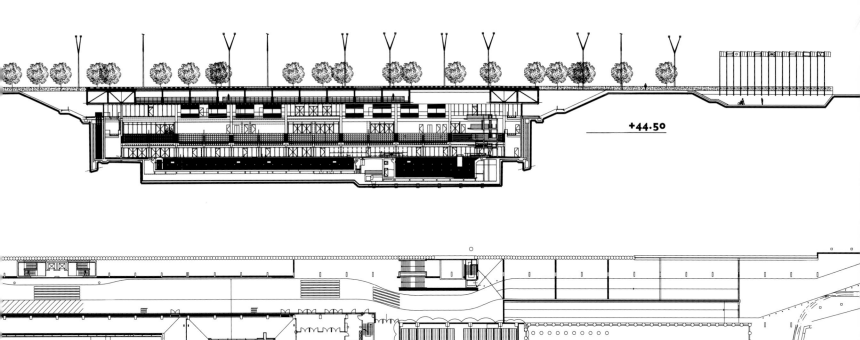

+44.50

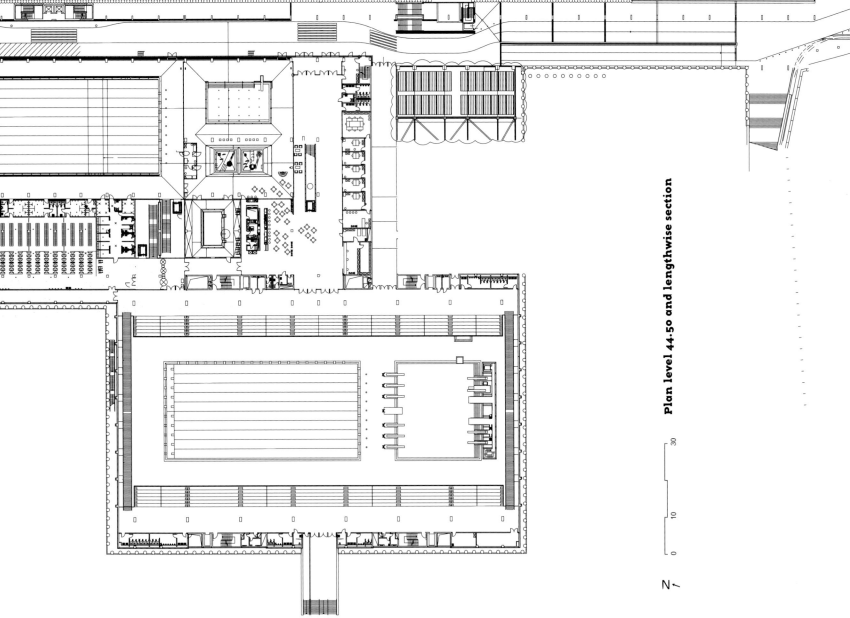

Plan level 44.50 and lengthwise section

30

10

0

N

1983

PAN XII competition
Trentenoult

National health laboratories
competition. Montpellier

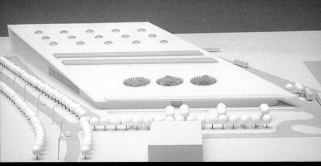

ESIEE –
École Supérieure
d'Ingénieurs
en Électronique
et Électrotechnique
built
Cité Descartes,
Noisy-le-Grand,
Marne-la-Vallée

SEITA distribution center competition
Marne-la-Vallée

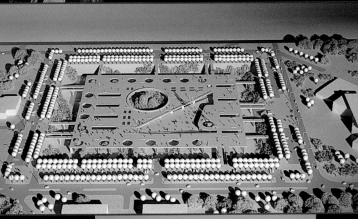

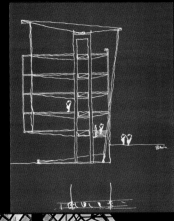

University
of Law and Arts
competition,
mentioned entry
Angers

Z.A.C. Chevaleret
study
Paris

Hôtel Industriel
Jean-Baptiste Berlier
built
26 rue Bruneseau,
Paris

STAG advertising
agency
built
28 rue Ponchet,
Paris

1988

Urban development
of the banks of
the Loire
study. Rezé-les-Nantes

Canopy for the F. Le Basser stadium
competition. Laval

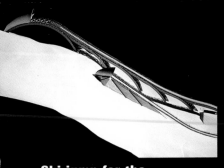

**Ski jump for the
16th Winter Olympics**
competition. Saint-Bon. Courchevel

**Head office
of Le Monde**
competition
Paris

Head office and studios of Canal+
competition. selected entry. Paris

"Hysope" development plan
study. Paris

Hôtel Départemental de la Meuse
built. Bar-le-Duc

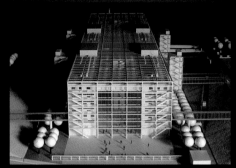

Hôpital d'Instruction des Armées Percy
competition. Clamart

Hospital and maternity center competition
Albertville

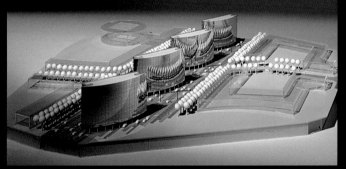

C.G.I. offices study
Villepinte

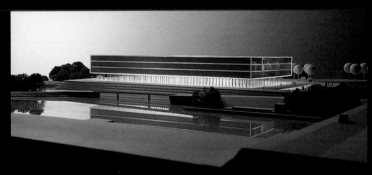

Palais Européen des Droits de l'Homme competition
Strasbourg

Technology school competition
Clermont-Ferrand

IFMA Institut Français de Mécanique Avancée
competition. Aubière, Clermont-Ferrand

**Steel fabrics
and by-products**

**ENPC-ENSG Écoles Nationales des Ponts et
Chaussées et Supérieure de Géographie**
competition. Marne-la-Vallée

Charles de Gaulle bridge
competition
Paris

"Le Louis Lumière" housing built
3 rue Chauveau-Lagarde, Saint-Quentin-en-Yvelines

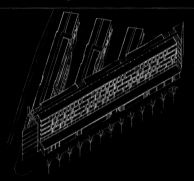

Gymnasium competition
Sèvres

École des Mines competition
Douai

1989

Z.A.C. de la Croix Blanche study
Bussy-Saint-Georges

Head office of Technip
competition
Rueil-Malmaison

"Les Balcons du Canal" housing ZAC Flandres-Soissons built
23-25 Quai de Seine,
Paris

ISMRA Institut des Sciences de la Matière et du Rayonnement
competition. Caen

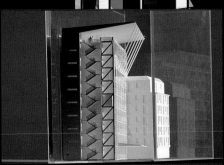

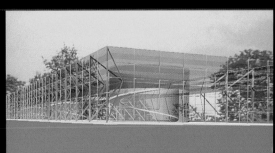

Porte d'Italie, offices
competition. Paris

Archives Départementales de la Mayenne
built. Rue des Archives, Laval

Head office of JC Decaux
study. Plaisir

IRSID – USINOR-SACILOR conference center built
185 rue du Président Roosevelt, Saint-Germain-en-Laye

Bibliothèque nationale de France built
Quai François Mauriac, Paris

1991

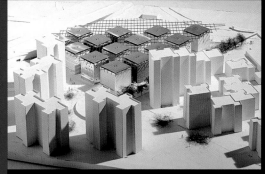

Business district study
Créteil

Alliance Française assistance to the client
Singapore

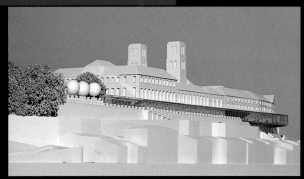

**Centre mondial de la Paix, des Libertés,
et des Droits de l'Homme** competition. Verdun

**Lu Jia Zui
Business District**
international
consultation
Pu Dong, Shanghai

Olympic velodrome and swimming-pool built
Landsberger Allee, Berlin

Urban development of the SULZER site
competition. Winterthur

Technal stand
built

Erol Aksoy Foundation competition

1990

ZAC Tolbiac-Masséna study
Paris

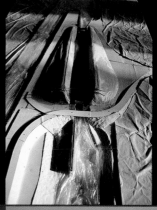

**Rhin-Rhône link
Bief de Niffer**
study. Mulhouse

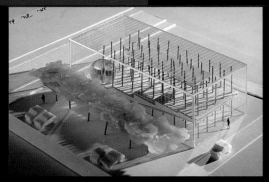

Vitrine de la Meuse en Ile-de-France
study. Marne-la-Vallée

1992

École des Mines competition
Nantes

**"Bordeaux
les deux rives"
Urban development
of the two banks of
the Garonne**
study
Bordeaux

Youville square
consultation. Montreal

1993

Wilhelmgalerie competition
Potsdam

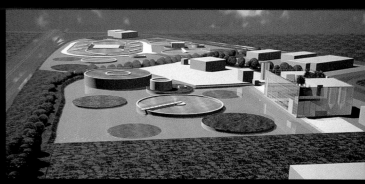

Neptune waterworks
Nantes - Petite Californie

Centre Technique du Livre built
Rue Gutenberg. ZAC de Bussy-Saint-Georges. Marne-la-Vallée

Vincennes zoo
competition,
1st prize
without follow-up
Vincennes

The Grand Stadium
competition,
1st prize
without follow-up
Melun-Sénart

1994

Villa Saint-Cast built
Côtes d'Armor

Salzburger Sparkasse
competition, 1st prize without follow-up. Salzburg

Urban development of the île Sainte-Anne
study. Nantes

1995

ZAC des Lognes study
Marne-la-Vallée

EDF poles for very high voltage
competition

Offices of the Ministry of Culture
competition
Paris

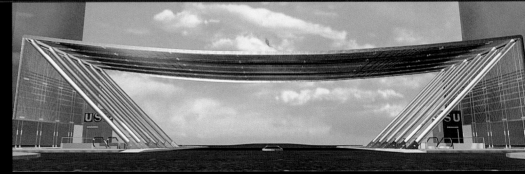

U-Bahn entrances competition
Berlin

Redevelopment of the UNIMETAL site
built
Caen

Place des Nations competition
Geneva

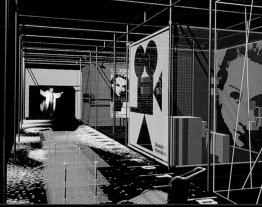

**Stand for the
cinema museums
of Berlin**
built
SIME 94, Paris

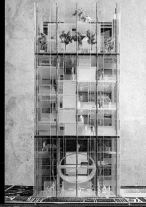

**Glass House
"Architectural Visions
for Europe"**
research
Düsseldorf

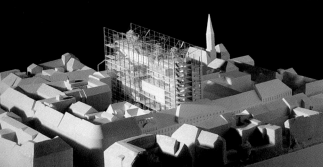

Hypo Bank – Theatinerstrasse competition
Munich

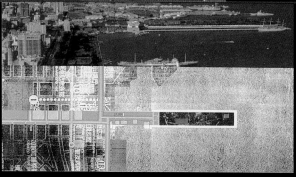

International port terminal
competition, Yokohama

**Furniture and
fabrics for the
Bibliothèque
nationale de
France**
built
Paris

**La Great Greenhouse,
permanent exhibition**
built
Cité des Sciences
et de l'Industrie,
Parc de la Villette, Paris

A20 motorway Brive – Montauban
competition

**Urban
development of
Storkower Strasse**
study
Berlin

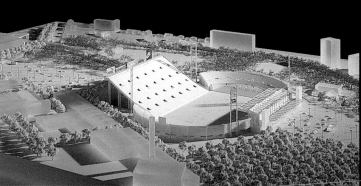

**Extension
of the city
stadium**
competition
Marseilles

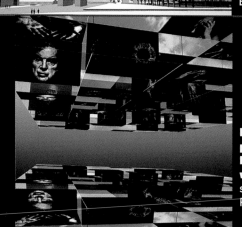

**Installation
project for
Francis Giacobetti's
work HYMN**
study
Paris

1996

ELEC'96 central stand built
Parc des expositions,
Villepinte

Urban lighting fixtures competition
Paris

Kolonihavehus installation built
Copenhagen

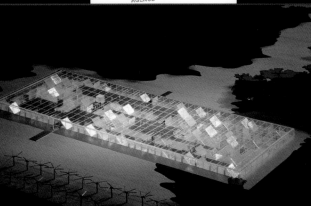

Kansai-Kan library competition
Kyoto, Seika-cho

Urban development of the heart of the Vieux Pays
Tremblay-en-France

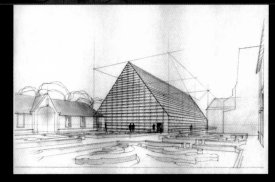

Theater competition
Château-Gontier

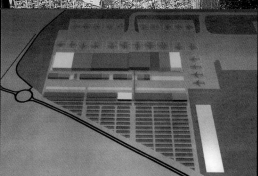

FEDEX European center competition
Aéroport Charles de Gaulle, Roissy

City project study
Marly-le-Roi

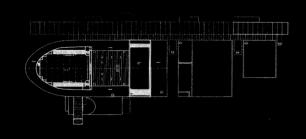

Requalification of Cargo competition
Grenoble

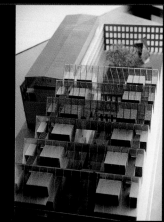

French embassy competition
Berlin

Town hall
study in progress
Innsbruck

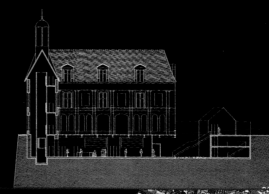

Courthouse
Feasibility study
Laval

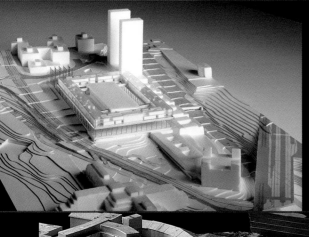

**Great extension
of the European
Union Law Courts**
study in progress.
Luxemburg

Centre des Archives competition
Reims

**Ministry of
Foreign Affairs**
competition
Berlin

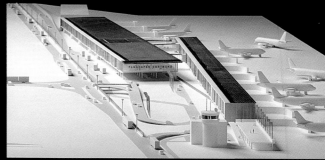

International airport competition
Dortmund

1997

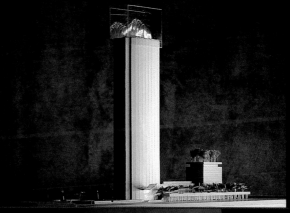

**Requalification
of the site of the
Tour Montparnasse**
consultation
Paris

**The Museum of
Modern Art**
competition
New York

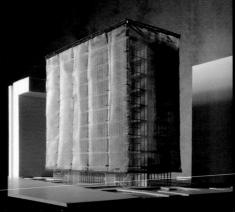

**Center
of Security
Politics**
study
Place des Nations,
Geneva

Urban development of the BLEG site
study. Berlin

Urban development for the Winter Olympics
study. Kitzbühel

Three hotels in the Antilles
study
Guadaloupe,
Martinique,
Guyane

Central mediathèque   study in progress
Vénissieux

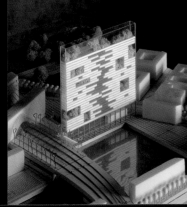

Lehrter Bahnhof tower
competition,
1st prize
Berlin

Public spaces linked to the tramway
competition
Bordeaux

Corsican port terminal   competition
Marseilles

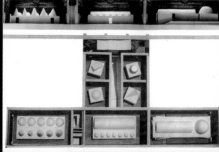

Set design for the collections from the Topkapi Palace of Istanbul   competition
Versailles

Central market
competition
Nancy

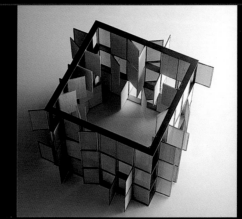

Pfleiderer pavilion
built
BAU 99, Munich

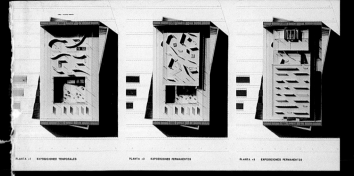

Museo Constantini competition
Buenos Aires

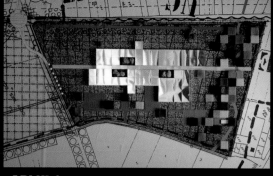

APLIX factory under construction
Nantes, Le Cellier

Bench for the WANAS Foundation
built. Stockholm

1998

**Messeplatz
tower**
competition. Basel

**Montigalà
sports complex**
study in progress
Badalona

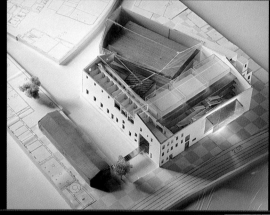

**IUAV – Istituto
Universitario
di Architettura
di Venezia**
competition
Venice

Temple of Mithra study
Naples

**Bercy-Tolbiac
pedestrian bridge**
competition
Paris

**Redevelopment
of the FALCK site**
competition
Sesto San Giovanni, Milan

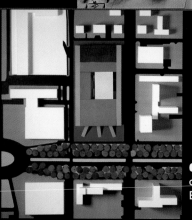

Convention center
competition
EUR, Rome

Dominique Perrault
Perrault Projets S.A.
Perrault Associés S.A.

Dominique Perrault
Aude Perrault
Gaëlle Lauriot-Prévost

Architects in partnership

APP Rolf Reichert (Berlin)
Bohdan Paczowski,
Paul Fritsch (Luxemburg)
Bernard Plojoux (Geneva)
RPM Architekten (Munich)
ATP Architekten (Innsbruck)
Pancho Ayguavives,
Xavier Gomà (Barcelona)

Engineers

Guy Morisseau (Paris)
Werner Sobeck (Stuttgart)
Tony Fitzpatrick,
Ove Arup (London)

Urban planner

Alain Charrier

Landscape architects

Erik Jacobsen
Confluences
Hardy Paysages
Landschaft Planen &
Bauen (Berlin)
West 8 (Rotterdam)

Economists

Paul Pieffet
Fabrice Bougon
Setra

Programmer

François Kerschkamp,
Gus (Stuttgart)

Consultants

ACV Acoustique
Alto Ingénierie S.A
Berim
Europe Etudes Gecti
HGM Guy Huguet S.A.
Jacobs Serete
Khephren
Technip Seri Construction
Technip
Trouvin S.A.
Sechaud & Bossuyt
Setec
S.I.R.R.
Sogelerg
SYSECA

Lighting design and acoustics

Jean-Paul Lamoureux

Scenographers

Thierry Guignard
Didier Onde
Alain Moatti

Photographers

Georges Fessy
Marie Clerin
André Morin
E.J. Ouwerkerk
Werner Huthmacher
Michel Denancé

Perspectives

Didier Ghislain

Models

Michel Goudin

Collaborators in the office of Dominique Perrault Paris-Berlin from 1981 to 1998

Daniel Allaire . Michel Alluyn . Claude Alovisetti . Emmanuelle Andreani . Fadi Ariss . Richard Asmar . Luc Augustin . Yvan Balp . Judith Barber
Thomas Barra . Christian Basset . Petra Baumgarten . Serge Bedoukian . Astrid Beem . Jean- Yves Beetschen . Geoffroy Belmont . Philippe Berbett
Pascale Berlin . Jerôme Besse . Jean-Luc Bichet . Isabelle Blancke . Gerhard Bodenmüller . Iren Böhme . Louis-Olivier Bonay . Yves Bour
Dieter Brandt . Geert Buelens . Daniela Burkardt . Jacques Cadilhac . Jean-Francois Candeille . Antoine Casanova . Rainer Centmayer
Hristo Chinkov . Gabriel Choukroun . Hervé Cividido . Fabienne Commessie . Marie Laure Comon . Yves Conan . Françoise Coulon
Constantin Coursaris . Sandrine Courvoisier . Nathalie Cozic . Patrick Crémel . Griet Daels . Luciano D'Aliésio . Armando D'Angelo Sante
Anne-Mie Depuydt . Olivier Desaleux . Francois Dessèmme . Alexander Dierendonck . Hélène Dittgen . Sandrine Diximus . Renaud Djian
Nicolaus Dohrn . Tatiana Dor . Céline Dos Santos . Christine Dos Santos . Laurent Ducourtieux . Bénédicte Duhamel . Antoine Durand
Marie-France Dussaussois . Peter Edward . Alejandro Epstein Patrick Fagnoni . Jérôme Farigoule . Pierre Farkas . Valérie Faugeras
Laura Ferreira-Sheehan . Evelyne Ferté . Mathias Fritsch . Corinna Fuhrer Dominique Gagnon . Laurent Garczynski . Shéhérazade Garman
Maxime Gaspérini . Catriona Gatheral . Jordan Geiger .Pablo Gil . François Gillet Reto Gmür . Nilberto Gomes De Souza . Frank Görge
Philippe Grégoire . Ulf Grosse . Claire Grossel . Frédérick Guy . Serge Guyon . Kristina Hahn . Michael Halter . Evelyn Hendreich . Reiner Herkt
Alfred Heude . Britta Hohmann . Jean-Jacques Hubert . Helmut Hutter . Dominique Jauvin . Holm Jellonek . Hildegard Jiouo . Caroline Joncourt
Christelle Julien . Olivier Jumeau . Anne Kaplan . Günter Katherl . Mahmut Kemiksiz . Wolfgang Keuthage . Karin Kuhn . Abdelkrim Karkach
Anette Klatt . Bradley Kligerman . François Koch . Victoria Koppenwallner . Rolf Koppermann . Roman J. Koschuth . Milana Kosovac
Angelica Kunkler . Martin Kursched . Corinne Lafon . Maryvonne Lanco . Catherine Lanot . Gaëlle Lauriot-Prévost . Jean-Jacques Le Berre
Zhi Jian Lin . Olivier Lidon . Christine Lelong . Philippe Le Moal . Ralf Levedag . Andy Lockyer . Frédéric Louison . Thierry Louvieaux
Nathalie Luyet . Gwenaëlle Manach . Yves Massardier . Patrice Marchand . Isabelle Marques . Philip Mellor-Ribet . Josiane Mettoudi
Thierry Meunier . Franck Michigan . Stéphane Monfort . Guy Morisseau . Jacques Moussafir . Thomas Mürrle . Heinrich Nau . Federico Neder
Ilga Nelles . Konstanze Neuerburg . Stéphanie Nichols . Carlos Nogueira de Diego . Yashuito Ohta . Camille Olsen . Patrick Pailloux . Sylvie Passon
Aude Perrault . Monika Pfretzschner . Valérie Phung . Corinne Pierre . Geoffroy Piot . Natalie Plagaro-Cowee . Patricia Pluns . Marcel Portefaix
Guillaume Potel . Rosa Précigout . Odile Prigent . René Provost . René Puybonnieux . Andrée Quignon . Sara Quintanilha . Neil Rawson . James Read
Martine Recchia . Ute Reh . Birgit Relsinger . François Revel . Martina Rhür . Martine Rigaud . Manuel Rigaut .Gilles Roquelaure . Hella Rolfes
Bernard Ropa . Marcos Roque . Dani Rossello Diez . Frédérique Roussel . Manfred Rudolph . Charlotte Russell . Anne Claire Saby . Eric Saillard
Antoine Santiard . Carola Schleiff . Cornelia Schmitt . Katrin Schmitt . Achim Schneider . Jeffery Schofield . Kurt Schuessler . Pierre-Yves Schulz
Karin Schumann . Jean-Christophe Schving . Nicolas Schwager . Xavier Simon . Claire Sion Christine Sohn . Anne Speicher . Elisabeth Stiefel
Daniela Stifter . Nicolas Tanquerel . Jan Taschschingkong . Dan Teodorici . Jérôme Thibault . Jacqueline Thirion . Veronika Tietmeyer . Yvonne Tietz
Olivier Tinel . Dominique Tirard . Catherine Todaro . Patricia Tolentino . Catherine Toporkoff . Jacques Touchefeu . André Toulouze
Jeanne Tronquoy . Anna Ugolini . Marie Urien . Jerden Van der Goot . Louis Van-Oost . Roland Vastra . Richard Veïth . Peter Verstraete . Carole Vilet
Nora Vorderwinkler . Blin Vose . Inge Waes . Rita Wagner . Brian Wait . Birgitt Wasner . Karim Wat . Julian Webb . Tamara Wehner
Gebhard Weißenhorn . Patricia Westerburg . Antoine Weygand . Christian Wimmer . Nichola Woolfenden . Magali Zuercher